Police Reform
Moving From Slogans
to
Solutions

Edward Zaccaro

Police Reform: Moving From Slogans to Solutions

About the Author

Ed lives outside of Dubuque, Iowa, with his wife Sara. He has been involved in various areas of education since graduating from Oberlin College in 1974. Ed holds a Masters degree in gifted education from the University of Northern Iowa and has presented at state and national conferences in the areas of mathematics and gifted education.

All rights reserved. Copyright ©2021 Edward Zaccaro

No part of this book may be reproduced or transmitted in any form, including photo-copying, except as may be expressly permitted by the Copyright Act of 1976. Requests for permission should be addressed to:

Hickory Grove Press
3151 Treeco Lane Bellevue, Iowa 52031
E-mail: challengemath@aol.com
Website: www.challengemath.com
Library of Congress Control Number: 2021910420

ISBN 10: 0-9854725-5-3
ISBN 13: 978-0-9854725-5-9

Books By Edward Zaccaro

- *Primary Grade Challenge Math*
- *Upper Elementary Challenge Math*
- *Challenge Math*
- *Real World Algebra*
- *Becoming a Problem Solving Genius*
- *The 10 Things All Future Mathematicians and Scientists Must Know (But are Rarely Taught)*
- *25 Real Life Math Investigations That Will Astound Teachers and Students*
- *When Math Matters*
- *Scammed By Statistics*
- *Now You Know Volume 1*
- *Now You Know Volume 2*
- *Pathways to Mathematical Understanding: Early Childhood to Middle School*

Police Reform: Moving From Slogans to Solutions

"Wisdom is knowing the right path to take. Integrity is taking it."

- M.H. McKee

This book is dedicated to my father, Luke N. Zaccaro (1924 - 1977) a mathematician, critical thinker, and philosopher who instilled in his children a love of life, fairness, reason, and responsibility.

Police Reform: Moving From Slogans to Solutions

"Policing is not getting worse — it is being filmed."

Table of Contents

Forward……………………………………….. 9 - 16

Introduction…………………………………… 17 - 36

Chapter 1: Pretextual Traffic Stops………….. 37 - 47

Chapter 2: Guns & Jaywalking……………….. 48 - 52

Chapter 3: Civil Forfeiture…………………….. 53 - 59

Chapter 4: Fines & Fees………………………. 60 - 65

Chapter 5: Police and the Bill of Rights………. 66 - 76

Chapter 6: Types of Police Encounters……….. 77 - 84

Chapter 7: No-Knock Warrants……………….. 85 - 87

Chapter 8: Drug Dogs………………………… 88 - 94

Chapter 9: Expanded Police Training………… 95 - 114

Chapter 10: Auditing Dash & Body Cameras……… 115 - 119

Chapter 11: Requiring Body Cameras……………. 120 - 124

Chapter 12: The Public Filming Police…………… 125 - 130

Conclusion……………………………………….. 131 - 138

Police Reform: Moving From Slogans to Solutions

Forward

Zayd Atkinson, a 26-year-old African-American man, was sitting outside his college dorm building where he not only lived, but was also employed by the college to keep the property around the dorm free of trash. John Smyly, a Boulder, Colorado police officer, spotted Mr. Atkinson and stopped his patrol car. The officer walked up to the young man and asked if he lived there. Mr. Atkinson, who was holding a trash grabber and a bucket, said he did and had a job that required him to pick up trash around the dorm. Even though the law is very clear that in this situation Mr. Atkinson was not required to identify himself to the officer, he provided his Naropa University ID when Officer Smyly asked to see some identification.

Officer Smyly, who should have ended his contact with Mr. Atkinson as soon as Mr. Atkinson provided an explanation of what he was doing and provided a college ID, insisted on confirming that he did in fact live in the building. Mr. Atkinson, who by this time was very upset at Officer Smyly's unconstitutional invasion of his rights and clear racial profiling, walked away and continued picking up trash around the property. Officer Smyly followed from a distance and repeatedly asked Mr. Atkinson to sit down and told him that he was obstructing a police officer by walking away. Atkinson refused to comply with what he perceived as a humiliating order to sit on the ground and continued to respond that he lived in the building, which led to Officer Smyly radioing for help because "the subject was being uncooperative and was unwilling to put down a blunt object." (The blunt object was of course the trash grabber Mr. Atkinson was using to remove trash from the premises.) The officer then warned Mr. Atkinson that, "You're probably going to get tased in a second, because you have a weapon." At this point the officer drew his handgun.

Dispatch called for 9 additional officers to aid Officer Smyly, which created a tense episode that could easily have led to the type of tragedy that has been occurring across the country. When the supervisor and eight additional officers arrived, they surrounded Mr.

Atkinson. (Some of the officers had either a handgun or a taser out when they arrived, but quickly holstered them when they perceived that the situation was not as dangerous as Officer Smyly had related.)

After residents of the dorm confirmed that Mr. Atkinson did indeed live in the building, Officer Smyly was told by his supervisor to return Mr. Atkinson's ID and clear the scene. Officer Smyly still appeared reluctant to stop the interaction with Mr. Atkinson, even though several dorm residents confirmed that he lived in the building.

After an investigation of the incident, Officer Smyly was forced to resign (fired). Mr. Atkinson went on to file a lawsuit against the City of Boulder, which was recently settled for $125,000.

https://www.youtube.com/watch?v=8ne6uRvQg2U

This episode highlights many of the current problems in law enforcement in the United States:

- How is it possible that an officer with 14 years of experience, did not know the difference between a consensual encounter and an investigatory stop? Constitutional law is very clear about this type of situation — Officer Smyly was engaging Mr. Atkinson in a **consensual encounter** because there was **no reasonable articulable suspicion of a crime.** Mr. Atkinson had a constitutional right to break off the conversation with the officer at any time.

- How is it possible that an officer with 14 years of experience would think it was wise to draw his handgun on an individual who was clearly not threatening the officer, but was only refusing to submit to an unlawful and humiliating order to sit on the ground. (Officer Smyly wrote in his report that he felt, "threatened by the trash grabber.")

- How is it possible that an officer with 14 years of experience would not know how to de-escalate this situation?

- Although it is difficult to prove, it is very hard to come away from studying this incident without coming to the conclusion that Mr. Atkinson was racially profiled.

For over 20 years I have been writing books that have dealt with mathematics, science and logic, so it might seem strange to see my name connected to a book on police reform — it shouldn't. My entire career as a teacher and writer has been focused on looking at problems analytically and searching for solutions. The high profile incidents of appalling police misconduct that are currently drawing an extraordinary amount of attention from the media and the public due to the ubiquitous presence of cameras are focusing and pressuring legislative bodies toward significant changes in the way law enforcement is practiced in this country. The emotion around this issue is intense and certainly justified, but putting forward effective solutions requires a systematic and methodical look at each area of policing that is deficient — determining why that is so — and then putting forward proposals that can, in a pragmatic way, correct those deficiencies. I hope this book will contribute, in a meaningful way, to that process.

Police Reform: Moving From Slogans to Solutions started out as an 800-word letter to the editor and quickly evolved into a 40,000-word book — the two stories I highlight below are the reason why. They encapsulate many of the problems with law enforcement today and highlight the emotion and desire for progress that I bring to this project.

Police Reform: Moving From Slogans to Solutions

December 2020   Windsor, Virginia

Caron Nazario, an African-American Army second lieutenant, was driving a new SUV through the town of Windsor, Virginia when a police cruiser signaled for him to pull over. Because it was dark, Mr. Nazario put on his turn signal and drove slowly for approximately one mile until he found a well-lit area at a gas station. Windsor Police Officer Daniel Crocker, who initiated the traffic stop for "no rear license plate and tinted windows," radioed that the driver was "eluding" even though the SUV was traveling at a low rate of speed and police are very aware that it is a very common and accepted practice for a driver (especially a woman) who is being pulled over to slowly drive to a safer area.

Another officer named Joe Gutierrez soon joined Crocker at the gas station. When the two officers exited their vehicles, they immediately drew their guns and pointed them at Nazario (who was dressed in his Army uniform). The officers shouted orders at Nazario — telling him to put his hands out the window and to open the door (a little hard to do at the same time). He was then threatened by Officer Gutierrez who told Nazario he was "fixin to ride the lightning," a reference to getting tased. When Mr. Nazario said he was scared to get out, Gutierrez responded, "Yeah, you should be."

When the officers tried to pull Nazario out of the vehicle, he asked them to please call a police supervisor. In response, Officer Gutierrez stepped back and pepper sprayed Nazario several times. As Mr. Nazario stepped out of his vehicle, Officer Gutierrez knocked him to the ground and Mr. Nazario was then struck several times and handcuffed.

Reading about Lieutenant Nazario's experience with these stunningly inept and unprofessional police officers is difficult, but please watch the video at the link below for a full understanding of the incident. These officers failed miserably in their understanding and implementation of appropriate policing. The fact that they treated this unnecessary and trivial traffic stop as a high risk felony interdiction is not only inexcusable, but because they repeatedly assaulted Lieutenant Nazario, their actions were likely criminal offenses. Lieutenant Nazario recently filed a lawsuit against both officers and the Windsor Police Department. The appalling actions of their officers will in all likelihood cost the taxpayers of Windsor a substantial amount of money.

Note: The reason for the traffic stop was a missing license plate, but Officer Crocker's body camera clearly shows a cardboard license plate, the kind that is often used on new cars, taped in the rear window.

Lieutenant Nazario's very dangerous traffic stop:

https://www.youtube.com/watch?v=RlS8ht3PERs

June 2020   Loveland, Colorado

Karen Garner, a 73-year-old woman who suffers from dementia and sensory aphasia, stepped outside of her local Walmart with a soda, a candy bar, a t-shirt, and some wipe refills. An employee asked her to return to the store because she did not pay for the items. When she re-entered the store, she asked to be able to pay for the items, but her request was denied. (It is important to know that forgetting to pay at stores is a well-known symptom of dementia.)

A Walmart employee then called police to report Garner's attempted shoplifting. Three Loveland, Colorado police officers soon arrived and intercepted Ms. Garner as she walked in a field next to the road toward her home — a short distance from the Walmart. One officer asked why she did not stop walking when she saw the police officer was following her in a patrol car with his lights and sirens activated. In response,

Ms. Garner shrugged, turned slightly, and then continued walking with the wild flowers that she had picked clutched tightly in her hand.

The officer then dramatically escalated the interaction by grabbing one of her arms and forcing it behind her back. He then pushed the 80-pound, very frail woman to the ground and not only handcuffed her, but also hogtied her. Karen Garner became very confused and could only repeat, "I am going home." — "I am going home." — "I am going home." When she asked what was happening, the officer explained, "I told you to stop. You don't get to act this way."

During her traumatic arrest on suspicion of attempting to shoplift $13.88 worth of items from a Walmart, Ms. Garner, who **has dementia and weighs 80 pounds,** suffered a dislocated shoulder, a broken arm and other injuries. In the lawsuit filed against the Loveland Police, Ms. Garner's lawyer explained that after she was seriously injured during her arrest, she was not provided with medical care or given mental health assistance. "Instead, the officers handcuffed her to a cell at the station for over two hours, keeping her isolated and terrified, in extreme pain, and then deposited her at the Larimer County jail where they lied and said she was uninjured, which ensured she continued to not receive medical treatment for another two hours. What little freedom and happiness Ms. Garner enjoyed in her life as an elderly adult with declining mental health was, on June 26, 2020, recklessly and deliberately obliterated by the Loveland Police Department." Garner's attorney also reported that since her arrest the previous summer, "she has become withdrawn, depressed, afraid to go outdoors, and that she needs help getting dressed and showering because she has lost most functional use of her left arm."

The actions of the Loveland police officers who were involved in this cruel, unforgivable act clearly had no humility and were lacking even a modicum of common sense. They were unable to grasp the most basic and rudimentary understanding of how to treat a vulnerable, cognitively impaired member of the community. If they treated a terrified, elderly 80-pound woman with dementia in this way, imagine how they treat other citizens.

Breaking news: Recently released video from the Loveland Police Department shows that while Ms. Garner sat in a jail cell, handcuffed to a bench and suffering from the pain of a dislocated shoulder and a broken arm, the arresting officers were sitting a few feet away watching body camera video of the arrest laughing and fist-bumping each other. As they continued to discuss the arrest, the officers can be heard saying:

- "That went well"
- "I think we crushed it."
- "This is great ... I love it"
- "Did you hear the pop?" (This was the moment Ms. Garner's shoulder dislocated or her arm broke.)

Almost a year after Ms. Garner's arrest, the officers were finally fired or forced to resign because of the public outcry after the videos were released.

Bodycam video footage showing Loveland officers detaining Garner: https://www.youtube.com/watch?v=gPPuD9V2Dmw

Video showing officers discussing the arrest of Ms. Garner:

https://www.youtube.com/watch?v=SmtxTWTTdC4

These two stories show some of the consequences of inadequate training and highlight several policing deficiencies that must be immediately addressed.

- Lack of weapons use training
- Lack of mental health awareness in policing
- Need for compassion, common sense and maturity

Police Reform: Moving From Slogans to Solutions

- Inability to de-escalate an interaction

- Racial profiling and pretextual traffic stops

Mandatory training for police officers in the United States is approximately 750 hours. Training to become a hairdresser in the United States requires 2000 hours. Something is seriously wrong.

Introduction

Millions of Americans — especially members of minority communities, are expressing outrage and frustration as incidents of appalling police misconduct continue to occur on a regular basis. In addition, many members of law enforcement and their supporters are also extremely upset and believe that police have been unjustly painted with a broad brush and are being unfairly demonized. The emotion from both sides is understandable, but if that passion is not eventually channeled into productive proposals for changes to law enforcement and how it is practiced in the United States, the polarization that is inherent in anger is likely to cause the reform movement to drift into areas that are at best ineffective and at worst counterproductive.

With the need for bold and definitive movement toward solutions to law enforcement misconduct so apparent, it is beyond frustrating to see and hear media coverage that seems to focus on handwringing and ineffectual slogans that are circulating in response to the abhorrent abuse in which some members of law enforcement engage. The anger and passion that lead to slogans such as, *Black Lives Matter, Blue Lives Matter, All Lives Matter,* and *Defund the Police* can easily be justified, but it is important to remember that each incident of abusive behavior by police officers is not only harmful to the individuals impacted by that abuse, but also contributes to the deterioration of public trust — which can lead to generations of cynicism and suspicion. Because of this, it is imperative that we as a country quickly move beyond chants and slogans to an emphasis on putting forward reasonable, pragmatic solutions that might finally address the real issues of police misconduct that include, but go far beyond, racial profiling.

The intent of this book is not to present a dispassionate and balanced review of the quality of law enforcement in the United States. On the contrary, the objective of this analysis is only to point out areas where improvement is needed, and then propose practical and effective changes to policies and training that are currently deficient. There may be criticism that this book is not a balanced view of the good and bad of current law enforcement. If so, I would fully agree with that sentiment, but I would also add that it was not my intention to write such a book. I have no way of knowing whether 90% of police departments across the country act professionally and ethically or if the percentage is closer to 20%. My guess is that the proportion is somewhere between 75% and 85%, but whether it is 20% or 90% is not relevant to what will be discussed here.

An appropriate analogy to this book's scrutiny of law enforcement might be a study of the Titanic disaster. Those who examined the tragedy needed to get to the bottom of what went **wrong** in order to make maritime travel safer. Because of that goal, researchers didn't spend a lot of time cheerleading for the hundreds of safe crossings that were being made. When the analysis of the mistakes and errors from Titanic's fateful voyage were completed, the information that was gathered and studied went a long way toward ensuring that a disaster of that scale would not happen again.

Because of the number of high profile cases where African-Americans have been the subject of horrendous law enforcement abuse, the focus of police reform for the past several years has been on racial profiling and bias. The statistics are damning and definitive — racial profiling is real and an area of great concern in law enforcement today. But because racial profiling and racial bias are both so ingrained in society and are therefore very difficult to eliminate, the 12 changes suggested here, while not dealing directly with racial profiling or bias, should lead to a dramatic drop in the occurrence of both as a byproduct of the proposed policy modifications.

The changes that will be put forward deal not only with how police are trained, evaluated, and ultimately held accountable when they do not meet a high level of professionalism, but they also include changes to specific policies and procedures that guide police officers each day as they work to uphold the law. Once implemented, this new approach to law enforcement should lead to a higher level of police "legitimacy," not only in African-American communities, but in all communities. The public's perceptions about the lawfulness and legitimacy of law enforcement is extremely important because police cannot expect cooperation from the people they serve if the judgment of the people in that community is that police cannot be trusted, do not deserve to hold authority, and that their actions are not appropriate to the circumstances. These changes should also make policing more effective and far less dangerous — for members of the community **and** for the police officers who are tasked with protecting that community.

The first step in the reform process is to accept that a professionally run police force is an integral part of a properly functioning society. The country was given a glimpse of the consequences of abolishing a police presence in June of 2020 when protesters were allowed to create an ill-advised "autonomous zone" near the city of Seattle's downtown. Protesters entered Seattle's East Precinct building and declared the surrounding area a police-free zone. The radical utopian experiment was often described as a large block party and police stayed away from the six-block area for almost a month. Several weeks later however, the first of several shootings occurred, and after two Black teenagers were shot and killed, Seattle's mayor had had enough and police moved in with riot gear and the experiment was over.

Law enforcement as it exists today is not perfect and although it is true that many communities would be better served if law enforcement had more involvement from trained social workers, psychologists, and drug rehabilitation counselors, having only unarmed therapists available is obviously not a viable alternative when dealing with armed assailants, gangs, bank robberies, mass shootings, and other potentially violent situations.

After accepting the reality that having only unarmed police is not an option, we need to approach policing failures in the same way we would approach medical care failures. If surgeons were experiencing operating fatalities at much higher levels with African-American patients or low income patients, no one would be talking about "defunding the hospitals" — they would be talking about ways to improve surgical outcomes. Likewise, if a disturbing number of hospital patients were dying from medical errors, no one would be talking about shutting down hospitals.

Those who are interested in reforms to law enforcement would be well-served to study the methodical, statistical approach of a pediatrician named Don Berwick who wanted reforms in medical care. His passionate crusade for safer hospital care was prompted by the publication of a report by the Institute of Medicine that documented the fact that preventable medical errors caused close to 100,000 deaths each year.

This report started Dr. Berwick on his quest to prevent unnecessary hospital deaths. He studied the statistics concerning patient mortality and challenged hospitals to make six distinct procedural changes that would likely prevent a significant number of those deaths. He determined that if a large number of hospitals agreed to implement his suggestions, over 100,000 lives would be saved in an 18-month period.

These are the six changes he recommended:

(1) Elevate beds after surgery and clean the patient's mouth frequently. Studies show that if a bed is elevated after surgery and the patient's mouth is cleaned frequently, lung infections are dramatically reduced.

(2) Prevent medication errors. Institute checklist procedures to make sure the correct drugs are prescribed and administered. Make sure medicines are transferred accurately when a patient changes hospital rooms, changes hospitals, or returns home.

(3) Ensure that evidence-based heart attack treatments are used (aspirin and beta blockers on arrival and then clot busters).

(4) Ensure that there is a timely, efficient and effective bedside response when a patient needs emergency care.

(5) Implement procedures to prevent infections caused by central line catheters such as handwashing and cleaning the skin with a powerful antiseptic. This procedure alone was estimated to have the potential to prevent 25,000 deaths per year.

(6) Prevent surgical-site infections — the most common cause of complications or death after operations. Ensure the right antibiotics are used at the right time. Ensure that handwashing rules are enforced. Clip hair at the surgery site instead of shaving, which avoids nicking the skin.

Dr. Berwick compared his changes to the checklists airline pilots are required to follow. Pilots do not have a choice as to whether they follow flight checklists and Dr. Berwick believed that doctors should not have that choice either. If the procedures he designed were done methodically and by the book, Dr. Berwick was confident that fewer mistakes would occur and a significant number of lives would be saved. Berwick signed up nearly 75 percent of the hospitals in the United States and after 18 months, a statistical analysis showed that the new procedures saved over 100,000 lives. Dr. Berwick had a dramatic impact on hospital safety by simply doing a statistical analysis to determine why people were dying in hospitals and then looking for evidenced-based interventions to prevent those deaths. (From the book *Scammed By Statistics*)

If our country, like Dr. Berwick, starts looking analytically at the current issues we are experiencing with law enforcement and then pivots toward a different type of policing, it will soon become apparent that the focus and demands of the public must encompass much more than accountability. Accountability deals with compensation, correction and punishment for improper and/or illegal police actions and of course should be a large part of police reform, but the priority and emphasis must be on changes to law enforcement that will make the need for accountability much less likely.

It bears repeating that accountability is important, but **should by no means be the sole focus of police reform**. Contractors who have buildings collapse should certainly be held accountable and liable for their errors, but building codes and regulations exist to lessen the likelihood of being in the position of requiring accountability from people in the construction industry. Reforms to how law enforcement is practiced in the United States should dramatically lessen the need for accountability because egregious police behavior would occur much less frequently under the proposed modifications that are laid out in the next twelve chapters. The following few pages contain a short synopsis of each chapter and each policy change.

Chapter 1: Heavily armed officers with guns, tasers, pepper spray, and body armor should not in any way be involved in enforcing minor motorist infractions that can be dealt with by sending a warning or a citation through the mail. Law enforcement priorities should be shifted to impaired driving, dangerous driving, motorist safety, and criminal activity. Before community leaders get too excited at the potential new and significant revenue stream, and before motorists panic over another government program that drains their pockets, there is an additional caveat to this policy change: *All financial incentive to give tickets or to fine motorists would be eliminated by mandating that all funds acquired through traffic cameras and mailed citations would be sent to the state general fund — they would not be kept by local communities as a new revenue source.*

Chapter 2: Heavily armed officers with guns, tasers, pepper spray, and body armor should not in any way be involved in enforcing jaywalking, littering, and parking laws.

Chapter 3: Policing for profit must end. (*Part 1: Civil Forfeiture*) The rules related to civil forfeiture must be dramatically modified due to the fact that current civil forfeiture laws allow the seizure of money and property without due process. In addition, in many cases civil forfeiture laws allow communities to use seized money to pay the salaries of the very police who seize the money, a disturbing and problematic conflict of interest.

Chapter 4: Policing for profit must end. (***Part 2: Fines and fees***) Fines and fees should never be used for revenue enhancement for a city or a community. After Michael Brown was shot and killed by a police officer, an investigation found that a significant portion of the revenue that was needed to fund the operation of the city of Ferguson, Missouri came from the writing of tickets for various infractions.

Chapter 5: The limitations and constraints that the First, Fourth, and Fifth Amendments have on police officers when they interact with the public should be as familiar to those officers as red and green lights are to motorists on the roadway. Because a surprising number of police officers do not know or understand the laws that determine the legality of actions such as requiring a citizen to present identification, there must be mandatory training as to how the Constitution applies when law enforcement personnel interact with the public. (For example: Passengers in a vehicle that is pulled over for a traffic infraction are not required, in most cases, to give their identification to a police officer or even talk to an officer.)

Chapter 6: Police officers must have significantly better training to ensure that they understand the differences and legal limitations to which they are subject when they take part in the three types of encounters police officers have with the public:

- Consensual encounter
- Investigatory or Terry stop
- An arrest

This additional training will help prevent law enforcement personnel from violating the rights of citizens guaranteed by the United States Constitution.

Police Reform: Moving From Slogans to Solutions

Chapter 7: No-knock or "knock and wait" warrants should **NOT** be used for drug seizures. Their use should be limited to instances that involve imminent danger.

Chapter 8: The use of K-9 units should be dramatically scaled back. It is an undeniable truth that police in some jurisdictions are using drug dogs as probable cause generators even though drug dogs, for a variety of reasons, are **not** reliable indicators of the presence of drugs. If a drug dog "detects" drugs in a vehicle, the probability of drugs actually being present is approximately 50% — a coin flip. When a car is then searched without probable cause, it is a clear violation of the Constitutional rights of the individuals who are in that vehicle. There is a simple solution to the inappropriate use of K-9 units that will force police departments around the country to immediately modify when and if they decide to use drug dogs. This solution will be discussed in chapter 8.

Chapter 9: Law enforcement today needs more training and better training. When becoming a hairdresser in the United States requires 2000 hours of training and the mandatory training for police officers is 750 hours — something is seriously wrong. The United States trains police officers for approximately 21 weeks, while many European countries, with much less violence and crime, train their officers for 200 weeks. When inadequate instruction is added to the fact that the United States has 5% of the world's population and 42% of its civilian gun ownership, serious problems are bound to arise.

Chapter 10: The body camera and dashcam recordings of every interaction officers have with the public must be routinely audited, not only to monitor the demeanor and professionalism of officers, but also to ensure that officers' actions are consistent with what they write up in incident reports.

Chapter 11: Every police officer in this country, from the smallest town to the largest city, must have a functioning body camera. It is often said that body cameras and dash cameras are there to protect police officers and the public. This is only partially true. The main purpose of cameras is to protect, preserve, and record the **truth**.

Chapter 12: Because court rulings have made it clear that the public is allowed to film the police, police officers must be trained to react to a camera in the same way they would react to a person watching them.

Very little attention will be given in this book to many of the highly publicized cases where individuals have died as the result of inappropriate and violent police behavior. This is a deliberate omission and I would like to explain why. These cases have already had an extensive amount of coverage and will continue to be covered by the national and international press. The intent of this book is to address the issue of how we conduct and regulate law enforcement, which is much more complicated than addressing the specific police behaviors that led to the deaths of several individuals who were being engaged by police because of trivial offenses or, as in the case of Breonna Taylor, no criminal offense at all.

Breonna Taylor's case **will** be discussed in Chapter Seven, which analyzes the dangers of no-knock and "knock and wait" warrants. Some of the other high-profile fatal encounters with police are listed below — along with the trivial "crimes" that escalated into their deaths:

Eric Garner: Illegally selling cigarettes

Michael Brown: Reportedly shoplifted a box of cigars. Michael Brown, who was not armed, was hit by six bullets. The officer fired a total of 12 shots at Mr. Brown.

George Floyd: Allegedly passed a counterfeit $20 bill. Died after being held down by police officer Derek Chauvin, who had his knee on Mr. Floyd's neck for 9 minutes and 29 seconds.

Walter Scott: Shot in the back five times by a white police officer who was fired, tried and found guilty. He was sentenced to 20 years in prison. Mr. Scott, who was African-American, had been pulled over for having a defective light on his car.

Philando Castile: A police officer fired seven close-range shots at Castile, hitting him five times. Prior to the shooting, Castile had been stopped by the police at least 49 times in 13 years for minor traffic and equipment violations. Mr. Castile told the police officer who stopped him that he was licensed to carry a weapon, and had one in his possession. He was shot reaching for his driver's license.

Breonna Taylor: Ms. Taylor was a 26-year-old emergency medical technician who was shot six times during a no-knock raid at her apartment.

These high-profile fatal encounters with police that have galvanized the nation were not anomalies — they were not unforeseeable — and most were the inevitable result of poor training, mediocre supervision, and an appalling lack of law enforcement accountability.

The seeds were sown when:

- Heavily armed officers think it is appropriate to escalate a "possible jaywalking" infraction into an aggressive tackle and arrest.

- Police officers think it is acceptable to point guns at a car with a young man, a pregnant woman, a one-year-old, and a four-year-old and yell — "I'm going to put a cap in your fucking head!" — all because the 4-year-old might have shoplifted a cheap doll from a local Dollar Store. (They were African-American.)

- Nine police officers think it is acceptable to handcuff a 9-year-old African-American girl and then pepper spray her in the face because "she was being difficult."

- Five police cruisers and five police officers with guns drawn were needed to "apprehend" a submissive, frightened, unarmed young Black man who drove two extra blocks to his grandmother's house when a police officer tried to pull him over because he "did not stop completely" at a stop sign.

- A Black real estate agent and his client entered a house that was for sale — using the real estate agent's key. Minutes later they were forced out of the house at gunpoint by nine armed police officers because "we got a call" about two Black men entering a vacant house.

- Police officers think it is acceptable to tackle, arrest, and take to jail an 18-year-old African-American who was walking home after he finished his late shift at Walmart because "they were worried about him" and he did not want to stop and talk to them.

Before we discuss ways to improve law enforcement, the following two case studies will help the reader understand the depth of anger and disenfranchisement many in communities across the country feel toward law enforcement — especially those in Black communities.

Case Study

2015 Washington D.C.
(Story from WUSA9 News)

Vashti Sherrod, an upper middle class, African-American 76-year-old churchgoing grandmother of two, and her husband Gene Sherrod were sitting in their Mercedes when an SUV backed into them, causing minor damage. As typically happens after a minor accident, both parties exchanged information, but then tempers flared and the discussion turned heated. The driver of the SUV eventually left.

Seven hours later, the driver of the SUV called the D.C. Metropolitan Police Department and told them that Mrs. Sherrod pointed a gun at her. When a detective confronted Mrs. Sherrod with what the other driver said, Mrs. Sherrod said over and over, "That is not true. That is not true. That is not true." She then told the detective that she and her husband have never owned, shot, or even held a gun.

Six weeks later, Mr. And Mrs. Sherrod were out for a drive in their Mercedes. As they approached the Library of Congress, District of Columbia Capitol Police pulled them over. Vashti Sherrod described what happened next: "All of a sudden, we heard police officers yelling, 'Stop! Stop! Stop the car! Stop the car!' And then I looked in the rearview mirror and there were at least three shotguns pointed at our heads."

Gene Sherrod, who is legally blind, also understood that they were in danger, "I was crying. I couldn't believe those long shotguns they were pointing at us." The elderly couple sat on the curb as police searched their car for a gun. Not finding anything, a detective asked Vashti Sherrod if she would be willing to come back to his office for further questioning. Because Mrs. Sherrod was upset and didn't trust the officers, she refused.

Approximately two weeks later, as the elderly couple sat in their pajamas about to retire for the night, police officers arrived at their home with a search warrant. With their pistols drawn, Gene Sherrod was put in handcuffs and Mrs. Sherrod was told to place her hands on her head.

Officers demanded they tell them where the gun was. The police repeatedly demanded that the couple "give them the gun" and Vashti Sherrod responded that they don't own a gun. According to Mrs. Sherrod, the police "tore the place apart" looking for a gun that didn't exist.

So how did a simple parking mishap, with no evidence of the couple even owning a gun — let alone pointing it at someone, turn into a situation where an upper middle class, elderly, African-American couple with no criminal record ended up being treated as if they were dangerous criminals? This is why:

When Mrs. Sherrod was initially questioned, shortly after the parking mishap, Detective McHugh of the D.C. Metropolitan Police Department headed up the investigation and checked with state and federal law enforcement databases to see if either of the Sherrods had a firearm registered to them. Even though they did not, Detective McHugh put out a high alert to local and national law enforcement about the Sherrods and their car. When Detective McHugh registered the alert, it warned officers that the Sherrods' car may have been involved in a felony assault with a dangerous weapon.

After the fruitless search of the Sherrods' car and home, Detective McHugh, who by this time appeared to be developing an unhealthy obsession with the case, issued a warrant for Vashti Sherrod's arrest. It bears repeating that he put out the arrest warrant even though **no evidence of a gun was found during both the search of the Sherrods' car and search of their home, AND state and federal law enforcement databases did not show a firearm registered to the Sherrods.**

Vashti Sherrod turned herself in to police at five in the morning wearing a Saint John dress with T-strapped shoes and then had her mugshot taken. She was then transported by police van to the central cell block downtown. Later that day Sherrod was released on her own recognizance.

Shortly after Mrs. Sherrod's arrest, Detective McHugh suddenly revealed he had surveillance video that backed up the SUV driver's allegation that Vashti Sherrod threatened her with a gun. Later though, in a sworn affidavit, the detective admitted that the video was not clear enough to see if Sherrod had anything in her hand. All that could be gleaned from the surveillance video was that Sherrod's arm was stretched in front of her body. Vashti Sherrod testified that she was pointing at the other driver while the detective said it could have been an indication that someone was pointing a gun.

Why was Detective McHugh so obsessed with pursuing this case? Local journalists requested interviews with both Detective McHugh and the D.C. Police, but both declined to answer questions. Vashti Sherrod did express her thoughts about why she and her husband were treated in such an appalling manner:

"She was white. We were black."

Mrs. Sherrod said that throughout Detective McHugh's deposition he mentioned that he believed the other woman, but never believed her. "I told him many times that I don't have a gun and we didn't do this."

When a grand jury reviewed the evidence against Vashti Sherrod, McHugh's case quickly fell apart. When the driver of the SUV met with prosecutors, her memory became murky. The gun shifted from a black semi-automatic to a silver revolver. The witness continued to waver, "I saw a glint of a metal object in Mrs. Sherrod's hand." The last straw was the revelation that the SUV driver suffered from mental health issues and that she sometimes suffered from memory lapses as a side effect of her medication.

In January of 2016, all charges against Vashti Sherrod were dropped. The Sherrods eventually agreed to a six-figure settlement to end a lawsuit they brought against McHugh and the D.C. Police Department.

Part of a judge's opinion in the case highlights the dangers of an out of control justice system:

This case illustrates the harm that may arise from even the most trivial traffic dispute, when the full weight of the justice system is brought to bear on that dispute. Plaintiffs Vashti and Eugene Sherrod and Defendant Diane Schulz were involved in a minor accident in the District of Columbia that devolved into an intense shouting match. Hours after the incident, Ms. Schulz reported to the District of Columbia Metropolitan Police Department ("MPD") that Mrs. Sherrod threatened her with a handgun. MPD Detective Phillip McHugh, another Defendant, was assigned to investigate Ms. Schulz's accusation. He obtained a video of the incident that allegedly proves Mrs. Sherrod's innocence, yet he used the power afforded to him by the criminal justice system to stop and search the Sherrods' car, search their home, and ultimately arrest Mrs. Sherrod.

The Sherrod's story from WUSA9 News:
https://www.youtube.com/watch?v=68VdrNu_oPI

Case Study

Summer of 2014   Grand Rapids, Michigan

James King was a law-abiding college student walking between his two summer jobs when two men in t-shirts and jeans began asking him questions. Although he did not know it at the time, the men who engaged Mr. King were part of a combined task force of local police and the FBI who were searching for a fugitive. The men asked who he was and he answered, "I'm James." They then asked if that was his real name, to which Mr. King replied that yes it was. The men, who still had not identified themselves as police officers, then proceeded to pin Mr. King against their black SUV and take his wallet. Because he thought he was being mugged, King tried to escape and was tackled. He was then choked unconscious and severely beaten. As he was being beaten, Mr. King pleaded for help and for someone to call the police. Passersby heard his cries for help and at least one called 911:

"Oh, my God, they're pounding him in the head! They're going to kill this man!"

The task force officers soon discovered that the man they had severely beaten was not the man for whom they were looking — in fact, he looked nothing like the fugitive they were intent on arresting. James King was a young man walking down the street who, like the fugitive, was white with a height between 5 feet 10 inches and 6 feet 3 inches — and who happened to be in an area that the fugitive was known to visit.

The illegal and violent actions of the officers as they attempted to find and arrest a fugitive might be more understandable and possibly forgiven if the fugitive was a rapist, murderer, terrorist, or armed robber. It turns out that the fugitive whom the task force was so eager to arrest was wanted for:

> **Stealing a box of empty cans and several bottles of liquor from the apartment of his former boss.**

You might think that the law enforcement officers who were involved in this debacle would be horrified, admit they made an inexcusable error, and then offer a large settlement to Mr. King. Well, that is not quite what happened.

A uniformed police officer who arrived at the scene of the altercation demanded that **all witnesses delete any and all record of the assault from their cameras.** The criminal justice system then closed ranks and shielded all the police officers who were involved from accountability.

Was anyone held accountable for this egregious mistake? Yes, someone was. The police immediately used the power of the criminal justice system to punish one of the people who was involved in this appalling miscarriage of justice — the person they decided to hold accountable was: **James King** Even though they knew Mr. King was not the fugitive for whom they were looking, they charged him with three violent felonies and the criminal justice system took him to trial.

What happened to Mr. King is by no means an isolated incident. Most people who are in his position are not able to risk going to trial or do not have the resources to go to trial and end up taking a plea deal offered by prosecutors. The people who find themselves in this situation, the ones who are damaged the most, are unsurprisingly minorities and the poor. Even though they might have done nothing wrong, as in the case of James King, they will usually end up taking a plea deal if it is offered. Because Mr. King had the resources to defend himself in court, he refused to take a plea deal and a jury acquitted him of all charges.

It is important to highlight and expose what happened to Mr. King because his case is a clear illustration of the appalling lack of accountability that often occurs when law enforcement violates someone's Constitutional rights. Mr. James did file a lawsuit against the officers to try to hold them to account for their actions, but the police officers' lawyers testified that the officers were entitled to several forms of immunity, one of which is a very controversial type that police officers have used to escape accountability for violating the rights of people they have arrested. This type of immunity is called **qualified immunity** and will not be discussed at length because of the complexity of the issue and the fluid nature of our courts' interpretation of how **qualified immunity** applies to different cases and situations. In a nutshell though, qualified immunity grants government officials performing discretionary functions, immunity from civil suits unless it can be shown that the official violated "clearly established statutory or Constitutional rights which a reasonable person would be expected to know." In other words, government officials can avoid accountability through lawsuits even if they make stupid mistakes about open legal questions, but **can** be sued successfully if they make **really, really** stupid mistakes.

At the time this book was published, James King has been pursuing justice for almost seven years. The Supreme Court took his case and recently ruled against Mr. King: *A Michigan college student hit a roadblock at the Supreme Court on Thursday in his claims against two federal officers who tackled and punched him after mistaking him for a fugitive. The justices unanimously ruled that a trial court's dismissal of a separate part of the man's lawsuit may cause his claims against the officers to be disqualified by the "judgment bar" provision of the Federal Tort Claims Act. But the court left a sliver of daylight for the man, James King, to revive the claims in the lower courts. (From SCOTUSblog: February 25, 2021)*

Mr. King's story: https://www.youtube.com/watch?v=HujPlUyTXRY

I want to make it clear that I am not claiming to know what it feels like to be racially profiled or how it feels to be the parent of children, who as they enter the adult world, must worry considerably more about interactions with police officers than I or my children do. I am a 68-year-old white male from a Midwest state and personally have had mostly positive interactions with law enforcement. I have been stopped a few times "driving while hippie" and have had a few ridiculous "fishing for a crime" or "pretextual' stops in the past 50 years:

- Not dimming lights 400 feet behind a vehicle
- Driving 58 mph in a 55 mph zone
- Touching the center line
- Not stopping completely at a stop sign

Because it will be referenced throughout the book, it is very important for the reader to thoroughly understand what a "pretextual" traffic stop entails:

A police officer suspects a driver might be involved in illegal activity, such as transporting drugs, but does not have enough probable cause and therefore is not legally allowed to stop that driver. No problem — find a traffic violation. This is a pretextual stop.

The law states that the police officer can only make a pullover stop if they observe a legitimate traffic violation, but ask any patrol officer and they are likely to tell you that finding a "legitimate traffic violation" is like shooting fish in a barrel. I am not a police officer, but I sometimes play the "pretextual game" while I am driving, especially on interstate highways. To play the game, just pick a car that you are following and come up with "a reason" to stop the car. It usually takes no more than two minutes:

- Touched the edge line
- No seatbelt
- Illegal use of a phone
- Touched the center line
- Drifted a little within the lane
- Something hanging from the rearview mirror
- Tinted windows   (This is a very common pretextual stop. A police officer can always stop a car to "check if the tint is legal.")
- Dirty license plate

To say that the power of a pretextual traffic stop can be exploited in unethical ways by law enforcement is an understatement. One of the most damaging aspects of giving police officers the power to stop almost anyone under the guise of a "traffic violation" is the significant erosion of Fourth Amendment rights that are often an outgrowth of those stops. In addition, when officers are able to use pretextual stops to pull over anyone who "looks suspicious," racial profiling is almost certain to occur.

At first glance, this book appears to be a scathing indictment of law enforcement — it is not. The intent of this endeavor is not to criticize for the sake of criticizing, but is a sincere effort to improve law enforcement through exposing flaws in the way it is currently run. I want to make it clear that I have a great deal of respect for law enforcement personnel who do their job professionally and honorably, and that our country owes a debt of gratitude to these dedicated men and women. I would also ask my readers, whatever their opinion of law enforcement, to please look at the proposed changes and their impact on police and the communities they serve with an open mind. All changes to law enforcement that are being proposed are advanced in the spirit of making policing safer, more effective, and more rewarding, both for police and the communities that depend on those police officers for a significant part of their safety, welfare, and security.

We ask our police officers to be willing to put their lives on the line in dangerous situations such as intervening in domestic disturbances, dealing with mental illness, apprehending armed individuals, mass shootings, gang activity, and many other situations that involve violence. In addition, we depend on police officers to respond to, and try to mitigate, issues that they might not be equipped or trained to deal with. As mentioned earlier, it is very apparent that without police, our communities would be much more vulnerable to chaos and criminal victimization.

Chapter 1

Because one of the most dangerous activities for police officers and private citizens is a traffic stop, all police "pull over" stops for minor infractions that can be dealt with by sending a warning or a citation through the mail should be discontinued.

It is absolutely stunning that we as a country think it is acceptable to use heavily armed officers with guns, tasers, pepper spray, and body armor to interact with motorists who have committed minor traffic offenses or have minor equipment defects. Not only is it inappropriate to have armed individuals dealing with such trivial issues, but it is also a waste of human resources. Would we ask emergency room doctors to also change beds or serve food in the lunchroom? Would we ask nurses to enforce parking in the hospital parking lot?

The minor infractions included in this proposed policing reform would include, but not be limited to the following:
- Broken taillights
- Having an air freshener hanging from a rearview mirror
- Plate light infractions
- Parking too far from the curb
- Touching the center line
- Minor speeding
- Stop sign roll throughs
- Tinted window infractions
- Changing lanes without signaling properly
- Wide turns
- Seatbelt violations
- Light dimming infractions
- A missing front license plate
- Talking on the phone
- Expired inspection certificate

Taking away the responsibility from law enforcement for immediately citing motorists in person for minor infractions would not only improve safety for both police officers and the individuals they have contact with, but would also dramatically lower "fishing" traffic stops by cutting the over 20 million annual stops currently conducted by police officers by at least 75%. Under this plan, and because the core mission of the police is to control crime, police would be able to redirect their attention to impaired driving, dangerous driving, motorist safety, and criminal activity. Of course there would be many nuances to this new approach. For example, a borderline yellow/red light infraction is very different from a motorist who barrels through a red light and endangers the lives of other drivers.

Motor vehicles are clearly an extension of our homes and intrusions upon our freedom to travel without interaction and interference from armed officers should be valued more than it currently is. If traffic cameras can detect infractions and send out notices, police officers can easily note a license number and send a warning or a ticket to a motorist for offenses such as changing lanes without signaling. It is understandable that the public might be very hesitant to allow a policy change to be enacted that gives the appearance of opening a floodgate of fines and fees arriving in the mail — after all, many communities depend on traffic fines for at least part of their budget and policing for profit is a significant issue in some parts of the country. In-depth recommendations to end "policing for profit" will be addressed in a later chapter, but before community leaders get too excited at the potential new and significant revenue stream and before motorists panic over another big government program to drain their pockets, there is an additional caveat to this policy change:

All financial incentive to give tickets or to fine motorists would be eliminated by mandating that all funds acquired through traffic cameras and mailed citations would be sent to the state general fund.

Police departments should receive their funding just as fire departments, schools, roadways, and other government agencies are funded — with gas taxes, property tax revenues, and/or general funds. In addition, all penalties and fees that are levied for drunk driving, reckless driving, and impaired driving would stay in the community to encourage the monitoring and reduction of those dangerous activities.

The following case studies highlight the problems that can occur when police are allowed to engage in "pull over" stops for minor infractions. The potential negative consequences for both officers and the individuals they stop can be significant:

- Violations of the Constitutional rights of motorists
- Injury or death to police officers or motorists
- Motorists being charged with criminal offenses due to an escalation of the traffic stop
- Police officers being charged with criminal offenses or being fired due to an incident escalation

Case Study

December 11, 2014   Victoria, Texas

Victoria police officer Nathanial Robison pulled over Pete Vasquez, a 76-year-old Hispanic man, for a routine traffic stop due to an expired inspection sticker. After being told the reason for the stop, Mr. Vasquez exited his vehicle to show the officer his dealer tags in the rear of the vehicle that exempted him from maintaining a current inspection sticker. Mr. Vasquez was upset about what he thought was an unjustified traffic stop, but instead of deescalating the situation, Officer Robinson grabbed Mr. Vasquez's wrist and appeared to attempt to put him in handcuffs. After knocking him to the ground, Officer Robinson tased Mr. Vasquez twice and then ordered him to stand up. (At the time, Mr. Vasquez was a 76-year-old man who was 5 feet 5 inches tall and weighed 145 pounds.) Because the tasing left him temporarily paralyzed, Mr. Vasquez was unable to comply with Robinson's command and testified that he was afraid he would be shot.

The Victoria Police Department conducted a four-week investigation of Officer Robinson's conduct and concluded that he violated three department policies: Conduct and performance, use of force, and arrest without a warrant. He was fired. Vasquez eventually agreed to a financial settlement with the city and intends to move on from the traumatizing incident. "The way I see it is they have to have a good reason to stop you, and I don't give them a reason to."

Officer Robinson was only 23 at the time of the incident, but even though he was in his first year as a police officer, the number of mistakes he made during this particular traffic stop was stunning. Whether the mistakes were made because of the officer's personality, lack of training, or a combination of both is hard to say, but let's take a look at how a properly trained and mature officer would have handled this stop.

After Mr. Vasquez was told that he had an expired inspection sticker, it quickly became apparent that he believed that the vehicle was exempt from inspection laws because of dealer tags. Instead of immediately escalating the situation, it would have been a fairly effortless process for the officer to call headquarters to check on the regulation. A mature response of "I am not familiar with dealer exemption plates" would have almost certainly led to a better outcome for both the officer and Mr. Vasquez.

On the other hand, the whole situation would have been avoided if the Victoria Police Department had a policy of noting the vehicle's license number and sending a warning by mail that the inspection sticker had expired. If that vehicle was exempt, then the misunderstanding could have easily been resolved with a phone call or a letter.

Video of Mr. Vasquez's arrest:

https://www.youtube.com/watch?v=Nt4lu7RiN4E

Case Study

May 16, 2020   Midland, Texas

A 90-year-old grandmother peered out of her window and saw her grandson, a 21-year-old Black man named Tye Anders, pull into her driveway. Almost immediately, she saw a police car pull in behind him, blocking the car in. Her grandson remained in the car for several minutes before exiting with his hands in the air. Midland police officer Michael Rosero exited his car with his gun drawn and pointing at Mr. Anders. Mr. Anders called out repeatedly, "Why you stop me? Why you stop me? Why you stop me?" Even though Mr. Anders was very clearly standing with his hands in the air, the police officer yelled out, "Show me your hands!" Mr. Anders dropped to his knees and then placed himself prone on the grass with his hands outstretched in front of him. His grandmother, walking with the assistance of a cane, moved toward where her grandson was lying as several other officers arrived with guns drawn. As Mr. Anders continued to lie motionless on the ground, a female voice yelled to the police, "Y'all gonna find any reason to shoot because he is Black." At this point, Mr. Anders was crying uncontrollably and saying "I'm scared — I'm scared — I'm scared — Put your guns down." Because Mr. Anders was so frightened, he was unable to obey the officers' commands to crawl closer to where they were.

As the police edged closer, Mr. Anders's grandmother moved toward him in an attempt to protect her grandson from harm and lost her balance as the police officer next to her tried to direct her away from the scene. She subsequently fell on top of her grandson. Mr. Anders was eventually handcuffed, placed in a police cruiser, and then taken to jail.

Mr. Anders's grandmother must have been terribly confused and frightened. She must have wondered what her grandson had done to bring five police cruisers and five Midland Police Department Officers to the scene with guns drawn. Bank robbery? Car jacking? Violent assault? Did he murder someone? She would quickly find out that the reason police tried to pull over her grandson was that he.....................

might not have come to a full and complete stop at a stop sign.

Overreaction does not begin to describe how outlandish and dangerous the actions of the Midland Police Department were that day. This example highlights the need to end, once and for all, all traffic stops by heavily armed officers for minor offenses. If the police officer who pulled over Mr. Anders that day thought the stop sign violation was worthy of a consequence, he could have easily noted the car registration and had a citation sent by mail. Of course, it is highly unlikely that Officer Rosero was concerned at all about the supposed traffic violation because it was reported that he followed Anders's car for approximately half an hour before the officer said he saw Anders fail to come to a complete stop at a stop sign. (No evidence of the traffic violation exists except for Officer Rosero's claim.)

Tye Anders's lawyer, Justin Moore released a statement regarding the incident: "Racial profiling and pretextual stops have been at pandemic levels in this country for generations. This incident falls within the age-old trend of following Black men and arresting them for fabricated reasons."

As a final note, Mr. Anders of course was not totally blameless for the escalation of this incident. When the police officer started his lights and sirens, he should have immediately stopped instead of driving the two extra blocks to his grandmother's house. On the other hand, why was a 21-year-old Black man put in that position when there is a simple alternative — a citation by mail.

An individual on social media said it best: "Why the hell do they need several guns, including a shotgun, to subdue a single, apparently unarmed, visibly afraid man that has already submitted and laid down to be cuffed who was pulled over for rolling through a stop sign?"

The escalation of Tye Anders's possible traffic infraction did not end there. You might think that the Midland Police Department would apologize to Tye Anders and his grandmother. They did not. Tye Anders was formally charged with a felony a month after being pulled over for "running a stop sign." A Midland grand jury indicted Anders for evading arrest with a motor vehicle, a third-degree felony. Potential penalty: Two to ten years in jail and a felony record that will stay with the young man for life. All for:

possibly not stopping completely at a stop sign!

Video of Mr. Anders and his grandmother:

https://www.youtube.com/watch?v=6aDCY4XPqOY

Case Study

May 17, 2019   Rock Hill, South Carolina

Denzel Dunham, a 23-year-old African-American man, was near his mother's house when a police officer by the name of Cameron Kirby signaled for him to pull over. Mr. Dunham quickly turned into the driveway of his mother's home. She was on her porch and witnessed what happened next:

"The police officer jumped out and he drew his gun," his mother said. "I mean, I was scared for my son because I'm seeing an officer with a gun drawn on him. He could have shot him."

Mrs. Dunham was startled and immediately asked why the officer had a gun out and pointed at her son. Officer Kirby then grabbed Dunham and called for backup saying the young man was fighting, was trying to punch him, and was resisting arrest. Dunham was eventually arrested and charged with disorderly conduct. The reason for the very dangerous traffic stop: **seatbelt violation**

Police Reform: Moving From Slogans to Solutions

After the Rock Hill Police Chief watched the entire exchange captured on Officer Cameron Kirby's body camera, the young officer was terminated and all charges against Mr. Dunham were dropped.

To reinforce how objectionable it is to have heavily armed officers involved with low level traffic offenses, let's look at an analogy that most people would find intrusive, offensive, and unconstitutional.

It is 6:30 in the evening and a family hears a knock on their door. When the door is opened, there are two armed police officers asking for identification. When asked why, they mention that your sidewalk has not been shoveled properly after the most recent snowfall and that you are being cited. The officers then go on to ask if there are any drugs in the house or firearms. After telling them no, they ask if you would mind them searching your home. After declining their request, drug dogs are summoned to walk the border of your property. After getting an "alert" from the K-9 unit, several police officers proceed to enter your home without a warrant and thoroughly search it. Because you are "agitated," you and your wife are handcuffed and taken outside as four more armed officers arrive.

This scenario is clearly outrageous, but is it any more outrageous than stopping a car for a "phantom wide turn" or an "air freshener hanging from the rearview window?" Of course home visits by law enforcement are more than justified and reasonable when there is evidence of criminal activity such as domestic abuse, guns fired or even loud music. But let's continue for a moment with pretextual home visits for minor offenses. Just as in trivial traffic stops, the police could theoretically use minor offenses like these to engage homeowners in searches for "illegal substances and criminal activity":

- Your sidewalk is uneven.

- An RV is parked illegally in your driveway.

- Your garbage cans are too close to the road.

"I just noticed that your dog does not have a license! I will need to see some identification... any drugs, firearms or significant cash in the house?"

Using pretextual home visits for trivial offenses is, of course, unethical and almost certainly illegal, but using minor traffic infractions to initiate a "stop and search" of automobiles where there is no reasonable suspicion of criminal activity should also be considered unethical and illegal.

These searches are an affront to the principles this country was founded on and should immediately be stopped. Ending investigatory or pretextual pullover stops for the listed minor traffic offenses by shifting to mail-based citations and warnings will have the added benefit of significantly reducing the amount of racial profiling. This shift in law enforcement philosophy toward keeping roads as free as possible from dangerous drivers would not only be a more responsible use of armed police officers, but it would make policing more in line with the rights of citizens under the Constitution.

In conclusion, 80 to 90 percent of traffic stops are unnecessary and have the potential not only to be dangerous to both police officers and motorists, but also have the potential to infringe on the rights of citizens to travel "free from government intrusion." America's founders first articulated the right to travel freely in the Articles of Confederation and it is a right worth defending. Stopping unnecessary government intrusions during traffic stops is a first step. The following is another case study where a young African-American man was shot and almost killed during a trivial traffic stop.

\

Case Study

September 24, 2014   Columbia, South Carolina

Levar Jones, 34-year-old African-American man, had already pulled into a Columbia gas station when South Carolina Highway Patrol Trooper Sean Groubert pulled up behind him without his siren on. Mr. Jones had already exited his car when Officer Groubert asked for his license. Mr. Jones tried to comply and checked his back pocket, which was empty. As he leaned into the car to retrieve his wallet, Officer Groubert drew his gun and demanded that Mr. Jones **"Get out of the car! — Get out of the car!"** *Levar quickly complied and pivoted toward the officer. Officer Groubert immediately fired four shots at Mr. Jones.*

While Mr. Jones lay wounded and waiting for an ambulance, he cried out several times, "Why did you shoot me? — Why did you shoot me?" Groubert replied, "Well, you dove head first back into your car." Mr. Jones survived, but suffered a bullet wound to his hip. And what offense did Levar Jones commit that put the officer on edge to such a degree that he quickly fired four shots at Mr. Jones as he reached into his car for his wallet?

Officer Groubert stopped Levar Jones for a seatbelt violation.

Groubert was fired two weeks after the shooting. He was later charged with assault and battery of a high and aggravated nature. Mr. Groubert pled guilty and was sentenced by Circuit Court Judge Casey Manning to 12 years incarceration, with all but five years suspended. Mr. Jones, who eventually settled his lawsuit against the state for a little over $250,000, released a statement saying that he "hopes this shooting will lead to changes in how police officers treat suspects."

The shooting of Mr. Jones occurred four weeks after the death of Michael Brown in Ferguson, Missouri.

Dash cam footage of Officer Groubert's interaction with Levar Jones:

https://www.youtube.com/watch?v=giaTWGjhTTM

Because one of the most dangerous activities for police officers and private citizens is a traffic stop, all police "pull over" stops for minor infractions that can be dealt with by sending a citation through the mail should be discontinued.

Chapter 2

Heavily armed officers with guns, tasers, pepper spray, and body armor should not in any way be involved in enforcing jaywalking, littering, and parking laws.

The following three stories not only highlight the importance of keeping heavy-handed law enforcement away from trivial offenses, but they also are tragic examples of the potential repercussions of inadequate training, racial profiling, lack of common sense and an inability to de-escalate tense interactions.

Case Study

2017   Sacramento, California

Nandi Cain, a young Black man, was walking home from work in the Del Paso Heights area of Sacramento in April of 2017. Sacramento Police Officer Anthony Figueroa, who thought that Mr. Cain might have jaywalked, exited his patrol car and confronted the pedestrian about the infraction. The officer followed Mr. Cain on the sidewalk and started an interaction:

"Can you come here, please! Come here, bud. Get your hands out of your pockets!"

Mr. Cain complied with the command to remove his hands from his pockets, held them in the air so the officer could see that they were empty, and then continued walking. When Mr. Figueroa continued to follow him, Mr. Cain questioned the legitimacy of the officer's attempt to stop him. Officer Figueroa replied, "You're jaywalking. You were jaywalking back there." Seconds later, Mr. Figueroa dramatically escalated the encounter by threatening Mr. Cain.

"Stop right now before I take you to the ground!" *(While issuing this command, the officer's hand appeared to be on his holstered gun.)* ***"If you do not stop right now, I will take you to the ground!"***

Mr. Cain continued walking as he repeated that there was no reason for the officer to be engaging him. Officer Figueroa continued telling Mr. Cain to stop and then ordered him down on the ground. At this point, Mr. Cain removed his jacket and told the officer he had no weapons on him.

"I don't have nothing. If you're a real man, you can take your gun away, and you can fight me like a real man."

Officer Figueroa then proceeded to grab Mr. Cain by the neck and slam him to the ground. Mr. Cain was repeatedly punched in the face and head as additional officers arrived. Eventually seven officers surrounded Mr. Cain, and he was told that he was being accused of jaywalking.

"What's that?" Cain asked. *"I looked both ways, wasn't no cars in the street. I'm a grown fucking man. I know how to cross the street."* Mr. Cain went on to explain that he was taught in the first grade how to cross a street and that he did in fact look both ways. *"I don't give a shit about jaywalking. I don't give a fuck about none of that shit."* Cain then told the officers, *"I've been having a hard fucking week, and y'all need to leave me the fuck alone! I'm tired! I ain't got shit on me! I just got off of work!"* Cain said from the ground, *"You going to be hearing from my lawyer and my boss!"*

After being handcuffed, Mr. Cain was led to a patrol car and charged with resisting arrest. After arriving at the Sacramento County Jail, Mr. Cain alleged that his clothes were removed and that he was verbally abused. The charges were dropped within hours of Mr. Cain's arrest, and he eventually settled a lawsuit with the City of Sacramento for over half a million dollars. (Because of Mr. Cain's lawsuit, the city now tracks and reports all jaywalking tickets and also has made changes to its use-of-force policy.)

This is a video of Mr. Cain's jaywalking arrest:

https://www.youtube.com/watch?v=vrfNwsolZDY

Case Study

September 23, 2020   San Clemente, California

Two Orange County deputies on patrol spotted Kurt Andras Reinhold, a 42-year-old Black man, near the Hotel Miramar at El Camino Real and Avenida San Gabriel at around 1:30 in the afternoon on September 23rd of 2020. The officers can be heard in an audio recording disagreeing about whether Mr. Reinhold jaywalked because he crossed the street at a controlled intersection. After deciding that he probably did in fact jaywalk, the two deputies initiated an encounter and one of the deputies asked Mr. Reinhold:

"Are you going to stop or are we going to have to make you stop?"

Reinhold replied, "For what? For what?"

One of the deputies responded that he was being stopped for jaywalking.

Reinhold, who was unarmed and also suffered from mental illness, was still not sure why he was being stopped and began yelling at deputies:

"For what? ... Where? Where? ... I mean, why are you stopping me? ... Stop touching me. Why are you touching me?"

The deputies then attempted to detain Mr. Reinhold by tackling him. As the three men struggled, one deputy repeatedly shouted, "He's got my gun!"

After a short struggle, two shots were fired and Mr. Reinhold laid lifeless on the sidewalk. The two officers attempted CPR, but Mr. Reinhold was pronounced dead at the scene.

In a strange and tragic irony, it was learned later that the deputies who stopped Mr. Reinhold were part of the department's **homeless outreach team** that provided information to the homeless to make the process of accessing services less cumbersome.

The fact that a mentally ill, unarmed man ended up being aggressively engaged, tackled, and then killed because he "might have possibly jaywalked" at a controlled intersection is beyond obscene. It is very clear from video footage of the incident that the two officers created and escalated the confrontation that led to Mr. Reinhold's death and these officers clearly lacked not only adequate training, but also lacked enough judgement and common sense to know not to aggressively engage a pedestrian over a possible jaywalking infraction.

This is a video of the two Orange County deputies' interaction with and the death of Mr. Reinhold that began with a possible jaywalking infraction:

https://www.youtube.com/watch?v=e064cJ-2gsw

Case Study

April 2020   Miami, Florida

During an especially severe period of time during the coronavirus outbreak, a Black Miami doctor by the name of Armen Henderson was in front of his home placing tents into his van that he planned to hand out to the city's homeless. As Dr. Henderson, who is an internal medicine physician at the University of Miami Health System, continued loading his van, Miami Police Officer Sergeant Mario Menegazzo drove up and asked the doctor what he was doing and if he was littering. After Dr. Henderson told the officer that he lived at the location, the officer asked for his ID.

Even though Dr. Henderson was not required to identify himself, he appeared to be willing to produce identification, but said that it was in his home. Home security footage shows that the police officer then escalated the situation by handcuffing Dr. Henderson and walking him over to his police car.

Relating the episode later, Dr. Henderson said that the officer appeared to get upset at one point because he wasn't addressing the officer as sir or sergeant. When Dr. Henderson's wife asked why her husband was in handcuffs, the officer responded, "Well, because he has an attitude with me." After Dr. Henderson's wife retrieved her husband's ID, the handcuffs were removed and he was released.

This case certainly has all the hallmarks of racial profiling and has sparked widespread outrage in Dr. Henderson's community, especially because of his stature, reputation for community service, and the trivial level of offense that the officer was aggressively investigating. Whether this was a case of racial profiling or not, it was a clear abuse of authority and underscores why Black communities often distrust law enforcement. (According to a Pew Research Center study, only 30% of African-Americans believe that police use an appropriate amount of force on individuals who are suspected of crimes.)

Two YouTube clips that show Dr. Henderson's interaction with Miami police officer Mario Menegazzo:

https://www.youtube.com/watch?v=G7TitTesxnM

https://www.youtube.com/watch?v=mxebsmN_t4M&t=82s

Heavily armed officers with guns, tasers, pepper spray, and body armor should not in any way be involved in enforcing jaywalking, littering, and parking laws.

Chapter 3

Policing for profit must be permanently ended (Part 1)

Civil Forfeiture

There are two main parts to "policing for profit." The first is civil forfeiture, where law enforcement officers or government officials seize property or assets from people suspected of involvement with crime or illegal activity — all without due process of law. The other is where fines and fees help support the very department that is deciding whether an infraction has occurred. (Because many communities depend on citations for a substantial part of their budget, infraction and citation abuse is almost guaranteed to occur.) Fines and fees will be covered in Chapter 4.

Scholars can debate whether civil forfeiture laws are ethical and/or effective at stopping and punishing criminal activity, but there is no debating the fact that the way civil forfeiture laws are currently written, they give police or government officials a direct incentive to take as much property as possible. Some communities even use seized money not only to pay the salaries of the very police who seize the money, but also to fund Christmas parties and other "extras" for those same police officers! This clear conflict of interest is obviously too problematic to be allowed to continue. Even if we assume that these laws are ethical and effective, we should immediately take away all incentive to confiscate money or property by requiring any property that is legally acquired through civil forfeiture to be *sent to the state general fund.* In addition to eliminating local incentives for seizures, due process of law must be added to the requirements before property and assets are taken from individuals.

The following case study is a dramatic illustration of egregious civil forfeiture abuse and speaks to the urgent need to reform this area of law enforcement.

Case Study

August 26, 2019   Pittsburg, Pennsylvania

Terry Rolins, a retired railroad engineer, asked his daughter Rebecca to take his entire life savings ($82,000) home with her to Boston and to deposit it into a new bank account for him. Mr. Rolins was going to use some of the money to fix his teeth and some to repair his truck, but the money never arrived in Boston. Before her flight to Boston with such a significant amount of cash, Mr. Rolins's daughter did some research to find out if it was legal to carry that much money on a plane. She found out that it was perfectly legal to fly domestically with a large amount of cash, so she placed the money in her carry-on luggage and drove to the airport.

After Rebecca went through security screening, her luggage was held by TSA because of the large amount of cash. She was then questioned by Pennsylvania State Troopers and then questioned by a Drug Enforcement Administration agent. Rebecca was not charged with a crime or arrested, but the DEA agent seized her money. Months later, after several frantic inquiries, the government informed Rebecca that they intended to keep her father's money through civil forfeiture.

Terry and Rebecca were outraged and fortunately were able to get legal assistance from an organization called *The Institute for Justice*. Together they filed a lawsuit against the Drug Enforcement Administration and the Transportation Security Administration demanding not only that their money be returned, but also that the government end the unconstitutional practice of seizing cash from air travelers without probable cause. After the lawsuit was filed, and without so much as an apology for the nightmare that Rebecca and her father were put through, the DEA informed the Institute for Justice:

"After further review, a decision has been made to return the property." The translation of this statement is: ***"We didn't know you had the resources to sue us and would fight to get your stolen money back — we know that we will lose in court, so we are returning your money."***

Shortly after the DEA's change of heart, Rebecca released the following statement: *"I'm grateful that my father's life savings will soon be returned, but the money never should have been taken in the first place. I can't believe they're not even offering an apology for the stress and pain they caused for my family. Without this money, my father was forced to put off necessary dental work — causing him serious pain for several months — and he could not make critical repairs to his truck. The government shouldn't be able to take money for no reason, hang on to it for months, and then give it back like nothing happened, which is why the lawsuit we filed will continue. No one should be forced to go through this nightmare."*

This is Rebecca and her father's story:

https://www.youtube.com/watch?v=hsre7IOUUJA

Case Study

Two instances of highway robbery (by police) in Humboldt County, Nevada

Number 1

Matt Lee was driving from Michigan to San Francisco with $2400 in cash that he borrowed from his father to start a new job. He was stopped by Humboldt County Deputy Dove for a minor traffic offense in Nevada. Mr. Lee gave the police officer his license and registration and as the officer was looking at the information, he asked Mr. Lee how much money he was traveling with.

Mr. Lee told the officer about the money his dad lent him and mentioned that it was in the trunk. A drug dog was brought to the scene and "alerted" on Mr. Lee's vehicle. In the subsequent search, no drugs were found, but the $2400 that Mr. Lee borrowed from his father was confiscated. The police officer who stopped Mr. Lee said, "I am going to keep the money because I have concluded through my investigation that you are traveling from Michigan to California to purchase drugs."

(Mr. Lee eventually had his money returned after a lawsuit was filed in federal court.)

Number 2

Tan Nguyen had $50,000 in casino winnings with him when he was pulled over for driving three miles above the speed limit by the same deputy who confiscated Matt Lee's money. No traffic citation was written and no crime was alleged, but the officer took Mr. Nguyen's $50,000 and threatened to seize and tow his car unless Mr. Nguyen drove away.

Tan Nguyen filed suit in federal court and had his $50,000 returned plus an additional $10,000 for attorney's fees. The Humboldt County District Attorney's Office released a statement after the case was settled saying: "The stop was legally made and the cash lawfully seized, but there were procedural issues."

Civil forfeiture is sometimes even used by the IRS. The Internal Revenue Service has been known to seize bank accounts of businesses that have made individual deposits slightly smaller than $10,000 based on a suspicion that the deposits were purposefully kept below the $10,000 level to avoid the bank's reporting requirement and therefore "might" have been an attempt to avoid income-reporting requirements. (The IRS calls this "currency structuring.") After public outrage over a number of disgraceful "thefts" by the IRS where they unilaterally seized millions of dollars from the bank accounts of small business owners, they were forced to revise their civil forfeiture policy.

A 2014 episode of *Last Week Tonight With John Oliver* has a very good synopsis of the problem with civil forfeiture laws:

https://www.youtube.com/watch?v=3kEpZWGgJks&t=776s

A multi-part investigation by a Tennessee News organization did an excellent job of educating the public about the problems with civil forfeiture laws in the state of Tennessee. In the highlighted cases, a drug task force whose department was dependent on funds from civil forfeiture seizures, was taking part in highway shakedowns where officers were stopping out-of-state cars and seizing money, including $15,000 from a young woman who worked as a housekeeper and was bringing money home to pay the medical bills of her sick parents. The professed goal of the drug task force was drug interdiction, but after many journalists looked into the issue, it became clear that the intent of the officers was to seize money, not stop the inflow of drugs.

https://www.youtube.com/watch?v=rJd4Q4u5cqU

Case Study
Tewksbury, Mass

Everything that is wrong with civil forfeiture laws is brought out in the case of an elderly couple, Russell and Patricia Caswell, when their local police (Tewksbury Police Department) teamed up with the United States Department of Justice in an attempt to confiscate and sell the Caswells' motel. The two agencies wanted to take and sell the Caswells' property because 15 out of 200,000 guests (fewer than 1/100 of 1%) who were staying at their hotel during the previous 14 years were arrested for drug crimes. The two agencies were attempting to take their property despite the fact that the Caswells had always worked very closely with law enforcement officials to prevent and report crime on their property.

*The Caswells were in danger of losing everything for which they had worked over the past few decades, not because federal and local law enforcement officials were trying to end drug use and pursue justice. No, the attempt to **steal** their 2 million dollar hotel was a classic case of policing for profit. (Steal is **not** an unreasonable word to use here.)*

The Institute for Justice, a national public interest law firm that fights civil forfeiture abuse nationwide, represented the Caswells in defense of their property and their constitutional rights. The trial took four days and the result was a complete victory for the Caswells. A federal judge in Boston dismissed the forfeiture action against them saying, "The government engaged in gross exaggeration of the evidence and did not have authority to forfeit the property." The judge noted that the Caswells took all reasonable actions to prevent crime on their property.

According to Institute for Justice attorney Larry Salzman: "Mr. Caswell did not know the guests involved in the drug crimes, did not know of their anticipated criminal behavior at the time they registered as guests, and did not know of the drug crimes while they were occurring. This outrageous forfeiture action should never have been filed in the first place. What the government did amounted to little more than a grab for what they saw as quick cash under the guise of civil forfeiture."

One of the most alarming aspects to this civil forfeiture case was exposed during the discovery process: There was a DEA agent (Drug Enforcement Administration) whose job description included **searching online for properties to forfeit.** After spotting the Caswells' motel, it is very likely that the agent researched whether there was a mortgage on the motel. (A mortgage makes civil forfeiture much more complicated — the Caswells' motel did not have a mortgage.) The DEA then went to the local police and inquired as to their interest in working together to try and take (steal) the motel. The objective of the seizing of the Caswells' property of course was to share the cash that would be generated after the motel sold.

This is the story of how the Institute for Justice helped Russell and Patricia Caswell keep their motel:

https://ij.org/case/massachusetts-civil-forfeiture

The government officials and members of law enforcement who were involved in these cases of attempted theft were acting in a way that was not very different from mobsters. One could even make the case that these individuals were acting in a more egregious manner because they were acting under the color of law when they attempted to steal money and property.

The four cases mentioned here are the tip of the iceberg of civil forfeiture abuse. This entire book could be devoted to problems with our current laws pertaining to civil forfeiture and it would still only scratch the surface of the clear constitutional violations taking place. Many people naively think that if they explain a situation — for example, if they explain that the cash is being used to pay medical bills — that law enforcement will always try to do the ethical and fair thing. Then civil forfeiture happens to them.

Policing for profit must be permanently ended.

Chapter 4

Policing for profit must be permanently ended (Part 2)

Fines, Fees, and Jail Time

Fines, fees, and jail time should only be used to deter crime — they should never be used for revenue enhancement by a city or community that pays the salaries of the employees who are the very ones responsible for issuing the citations and setting the level of fines and fees.

Speed traps and monthly quotas for police would end abruptly if all fines and fees were *sent to the state general fund* and each police department received their funding just as fire departments, schools, roadways, and other government agencies are funded — with gas taxes, property tax revenues, and/or general funds. An interesting outgrowth of a policy change where communities would not be allowed to benefit financially from law enforcement might be the disappearance of traffic cameras that have been installed to "deal with safety issues." My guess is that these traffic cameras, which have become a substantial revenue source in several communities, would quickly "not be needed" if the revenue they generate reverted to the state general fund.

The death of Michael Brown prompted a federal investigation *(The Civil Rights Division of the United States Department of Justice)* of the City of Ferguson Police Department (Missouri) that revealed the inherent dangers of "policing for profit." After reading the entire report, it is very difficult to come away without feeling that the incentive for the police in Ferguson was not the safety of its citizens, but instead, was the fiscal survival of the city and especially the financial survival of the Ferguson Police Department. A small part of that report makes the city's dependence on and the city's fiscal connection to the police department very clear:

The Finance Director wrote to the City Manager: "Court fees are anticipated to rise about 7.5%. I did ask the Chief if he thought the police department could deliver a 10% increase. He indicated they could try." The importance of focusing on revenue generation is communicated to FPD officers. Ferguson police officers from all ranks told us that **revenue generation is stressed heavily within the police department,** *and that the message comes from City leadership. The evidence we reviewed supports this perception.*

Anger toward Ferguson's municipal court and the way it extracted revenue from the poorest in the community was the tinder that set the town on fire after the police shooting of Michael Brown. In 2013, Ferguson's population was approximately 21,000 people and its per capita income was $20,472. Ferguson's number of nonviolent arrest warrants — 32,975 — was more than double that of any other town in Missouri.

One failure to stop completely at a stop sign, or a police officer lying about a stop sign infraction, often sent poor residents of Ferguson down a rabbit hole of fines, fees, court dates, and jail time. Look at the following case study of one poor individual's experience with policing for profit in Augusta, Georgia:

Case Study

April 2012   Augusta, Georgia

(From *Harvard Law Review* "Policing and Profit" April 10, 2015)

Tom Barrett was arrested for stealing a can of beer from a convenience store. Mr. Barrett was given the option of a court-appointed attorney, but because he could not afford the $80 attorney fee, he declined representation and pled "no contest" to the shoplifting charge. Mr. Barrett was sentenced to a year's probation and was fined $200.

Barrett's sentence did not require him to stop drinking alcohol, but for some inexplicable reason, the terms of his probation required him to wear an extremely expensive alcohol-monitoring bracelet. He was ordered, under the threat of imprisonment, to rent the bracelet from Sentinel Offender Services. (The bracelet would detect all alcohol Barrett drank, but there were no consequences for alcohol consumption.) The cost of the bracelet was:

- *$50 startup fee*

- *$39 monthly service fee*

- *$12 daily usage fee*

The fees for the bracelet, which exceeded $400 per month, went to the private company (Sentinel Offender Services). Because Barrett was unable to pay the bracelet fees, he spent more than a month in jail. He would have stayed longer if it were not for the fact that a friend agreed to lend him $80.

Mr. Barrett's only source of income at the time was selling his blood plasma, so he was unable to keep paying Sentinel's bracelet fees. "You can donate plasma twice a week as long as you're physically able to . . . . I'd donate as much plasma as I could and I took that money and I threw it on the leg monitor."

Because Barrett began skipping meals to pay Sentinel, his protein levels dropped to a point that he became ineligible to donate plasma. Barrett's debt eventually grew to over $1,000 and Sentinel obtained a warrant for his arrest. After his arrest, a judge said that he could stay out of jail if he paid Sentinel several hundred dollars. Unable to pay, he was jailed again.

Is this the best way to deter crime? Rehabilitate? Punish? The "tinder" that set Ferguson aflame is waiting in communities around the country. All that is needed is a spark.

Case Study
Eagle, Wisconsin

The Town of Eagle, a small municipality with 3500 residents, has taken "policing for profit" and "code enforcement for profit" to a new level. The town has teamed up with a private law firm - Municipal Law & Litigation Group - to use fines and fees for revenue enhancement. The private law firm, because its fee structure demands that violations be found and prosecuted, clearly has a vested interest in finding infractions and seeing to it that fines are levied and paid. The law firm has even threatened citizens with imprisonment if court ordered fines are not paid.

(The law is very clear on the issue of excessive fines and fees: Governments may only impose a fine for a code violation that is reasonable and proportionate to the violation.)

The case of Annalyse and Joe Victor highlights the clear constitutional abuses that occurred when the town of Eagle, together with Municipal Law & Litigation Group, poisoned their code enforcement and justice system with perverse financial incentives. The town cited the Victors for multiple violations related to the parking of trucks on their 10-acre property. The Victors quickly tried to come into compliance with the town's demands, but they were fined $87,900 — $45,000 of which was to be paid to the law firm of Municipal Law & Litigation Group. There was a court hearing on the matter, but the Victors were not notified, so they were not able to tell their side of the story. The town's attorney, in addition to pushing for an $87,900 judgement, asked the judge to impose a potential sentence of six months in jail if the entire fine was not paid. The Victors, who did not have the financial wherewithal to pay such a large fine, were devastated.

At the time of publication of this book, the judgment against the Victors was being appealed through litigation with the help of *The Institute for Justice*. The Victors are not only trying get the judgement against them reversed, but they also are attempting to stop the growing practice of municipalities hiring private firms to take over code enforcement. This practice is clearly unconstitutional because it not only runs afoul of Eighth Amendment protections against excessive fines, but because it also encourages an impermissible profit motive that is a clear violation of Fourteenth Amendment guarantees of due process.

The town of Eagle has not only been skirting the constitutional requirements of the Eighth and Fourteenth Amendments, but the town is also involved in attacking rights guaranteed to its residents by the First Amendment.

Erica and Zach Mallory, who own a small farm in Eagle, were directly targeted for speaking out against the town at Board meetings and on Facebook. Soon after they became advocates for change and spoke out on behalf of neighbors whom Erica believed were being treated unfairly by code enforcers, the Mallorys found themselves being targeted by the same enforcers against whom she spoke out.

Town officials went after the Mallorys for minor violations and eventually the couple owed over $20,000 in fines and fees. An email Erica Mallory received from a Board member proved that they were indeed illegally targeted and were retaliated against for taking part in core First Amendment rights:

"*I wanted to help you, but you just ticked off the Board with your comments at Board meetings and on Facebook and that wasn't good because the Board members voted with emotion to pursue enforcement.*"

According to the Institute for Justice: "The town of Eagle has weaponized its code enforcement to enable the town to punish local residents who dare to speak out against town officials." The Supreme Court has made it abundantly clear that it is unconstitutional for a municipal's justice system to be influenced by perverse incentives to raise revenue.

The town of Doraville, Georgia, a small suburb of 10,000 people just outside Atlanta, is another classic and frightening example of how policing for profit is now out of control. Look at the following facts concerning Doraville's use of the criminal justice system to generate revenues:

- Doraville budgets between 17 and 30 percent of its overall expected revenue to come from fines and fees issued by its police officers and code inspectors.

- Fines and fees bring in over $3,000,000 annually to Doraville — a town with only 10,000 people.

- A 2015 Doraville newsletter bragged that Doraville's court system "contributes heavily to the city's bottom line."

- Doraville issues tickets totaling more than $800 per resident annually.

- Some residents have been threatened with criminal offenses and the possibility of jail for simple code violations.

Policing for profit must be permanently ended. Fines, fees, and jail time should only be used to deter crime — they should never be used for revenue enhancement by a city or community and its employees who are the very ones responsible for issuing citations and setting the level of fines and fees. (Fines, fees, and jail time should also not be used to inhibit criticism of city officials.)

Chapter 5

The limitations and constraints that the First, Fourth, and Fifth Amendments have on police officers when they interact with the public should be as familiar to those officers as red and green lights are to motorists on the roadway. Because a surprising number of police officers do not know or understand the laws that determine the legality of actions such as requiring a citizen to present identification, there must be mandatory training as to how the Constitution applies when law enforcement interacts with the public. (For example: Passengers in a vehicle that is pulled over for a traffic infraction are not required, in most cases, to give their identification to a police officer or even talk to an officer.)

Police should never compel an individual to identify him/herself without reasonable suspicion that he/she **was** involved in criminal activity, **is** involved in criminal activity, or is **about to be** involved in criminal activity. It is very clear from police body camera evidence and additional videos from private citizens that thousands of police officers across the country either do not understand these constitutional requirements or they do understand them but are choosing to ignore them. All police officers must know and follow these constitutional requirements. If an officer does not have a lawful right to demand identification and a request is refused, the officer must not continue with the demand or attempt to intimidate or threaten the individual.

Case Study

February 16, 2021   Plano, Texas

RJ Reese, an 18-year-old African-American, was walking home after he finished the late shift at Walmart. Several inches of snow had fallen, and because the sidewalks were covered in snow, Mr. Reese was walking in the roadway. After receiving a call that police labeled a "welfare check," two police officers arrived to find Mr. Reese wearing a t-shirt, even though the temperature was in the teens. After making it clear that they were there to offer help, the police officers started a conversation with Mr. Reese.

"Dude, stop, we're trying to help you. Hey man, you trying to get home?"

Reese politely answered their questions, "Nah, I'm straight."

After one officer mentions that he is walking in the middle of the road, Reese responds, "My bad, I understand that."

After the officers ask if he needs a ride home, Reese tells them that he does this every night, he is fine, and he wants to walk home. After Reese stops walking, a female officer moves toward him.

"I ain't going to put my hand on a female, please don't touch me." Another officer then informs Reese that he is officially detained.

Reese responds, "No."

The officer replies, "Yes, yes you are. Put your hands behind your back. You are not free to go. The next thing you do is you're going to get a charge."

An incredulous Reese asks, "For what? My house is literally right there."

Reese is then handcuffed, walked to the police car, and taken to jail where he is forced to spend the night. In a stunning piece of irony, almost certainly lost on the officers who arrested him — **as Mr. Reese was being walked to the police car, one of the officers scolded the teen saying, "We were honestly just trying to check on you. Now look at where we are. You caused a whole lot of something out of nothing."**

Reese's mom best summed up the incident when she told the press: "He was arrested for something that he should not have been even arrested for. Walking home, in the snow, from work. He worked the late shift and he was rewarded with a night in jail. My child sat in jail for a whole night, cold, in a cold jail, for a whole night. After serving his community, that's what he was given. To me, it eats me up inside."

The police officers not only lacked the legal grounds to arrest Mr. Reese, they also lacked legal authority to forcefully detain him and even lacked the legal right to demand he talk to them. While the initial consensual encounter was certainly justified because of the weather and how Mr. Reese was dressed, the escalation into an unlawful and unprofessional investigatory stop and arrest was clearly illegal because the officers did not have reasonable suspicion that Mr. Reese had committed, was committing, or was about to commit a crime. To use the argument that because Mr. Reese was walking in the road was reason enough to detain and arrest him is beyond ludicrous. The officers in this situation failed miserably in their understanding and implementation of the differences and legal limitations that they are subject to when they have encounters with individuals. Mr. Reese's rights that the officers violated are clearly defined rights that have been enshrined and guaranteed in the United States Constitution and have been reinforced by years of case law.

Teenager walking home:
https://www.youtube.com/watch?v=5Peck717VqU

Case Study

March 2020   Leavenworth, Kansas

Leavenworth police received a call about an illegally parked trailer that was at the home of Robert Ennest. When they arrived, in addition to calling a tow truck, the officers walked up to the front door with guns drawn, knocked, and when no one answered, entered the house and searched it without obtaining a warrant.

The officers wrote in their report that as they knocked on the door, the door opened. Footage from a security camera showed that they were clearly not telling the truth. In the video, a doorknob twist can be clearly heard as one officer is knocking. Mr. Ennest wanted to know how it was possibly ethical or legal for the police to enter a home when the owners were not there — without a warrant. The department's response was that after no one answered the door, the officers made a judgment call and went inside the house to see if someone was hurt.

To add insult to injury, Ennest said the officers tracked mud throughout the house and his family ended up being forced to clean carpets, laundry and bedding. He added that because of COVID, his family spent the night sanitizing their home because their son is fighting cancer and couldn't afford the risk of getting sick. In addition, Mr. Ennest has a 12-year-old daughter who was home at the time, but fortunately was in a neighbor's yard. If she had been in the house, not only would she have been traumatized, but she could also have been shot.

The message from this violation of Mr. Ennest's rights is clear. Some police officers do not respect the need for a search warrant as the Fourth Amendment demands. To treat the limitations of the Constitution on their police powers with such frivolity is very disturbing and points to clear deficiencies in training and aptitude. There was absolutely no indication anyone was in distress in that home and the Leavenworth police officers who drew their weapons clearly knew that.

Police illegally entering the home of Robert Ennest:
https://www.youtube.com/watch?v=ld0sk5K-EbE

Activists helping the police understand First, Fourth and Fifth Amendment rights

There are currently several activist organizations in the United States and Canada whose purpose is to observe, document, and record police activity. These groups hope that monitoring police activity is a way to not only prevent police brutality, but also to hold officers accountable when police misconduct occurs.

Another slightly different activist group conducts sidewalk or easement audits that are meant to assert the First Amendment right of citizens to film from public areas. Their goal is to test and "teach" law enforcement about citizen rights and the restrictions and constraints law enforcement must follow because of the First, Fourth and Fifth Amendments. This type of audit usually starts when a property owner, police officer, or other government official tells the auditor, who is always filming from public property, that photographing their property is not allowed.

The less confrontational auditors will next tell property owners or police officers, upon questioning, that they are photographing or recording for a story or something similar. Police officers will often approach the auditors and ask what they are doing and then request identification. The approach by a police officer is, of course, the intent of the audit — to provoke a confrontation based on the First, Fourth, and Fifth Amendment rights of the auditor. The auditor then states that they are not required to identify themselves unless they are suspected of having committed a crime, are currently committing a crime, or are about to commit a crime and that filming from a public area is not against the law. After the auditor quotes the relevant law to the officer as justification for their refusal to self-identify, one of the following actions usually takes place:

1) The officer might acknowledge the rights of the auditor and end the encounter.

2) The officer may press the auditor for identification by insisting that it is within the rights of the officer to demand an ID. Many officers back down eventually, de-escalate the situation, and then end the interaction. Many officers then check with a supervisor to see if they indeed can require identification from a person filming from a public area. If their supervisor is knowledgable, the officer might learn something new about Constitutional law and its requirements and constraints when police interact with the public.

3) Auditors sometimes are illegally arrested by police officers for failing to identify themselves and then are charged with crimes such as obstruction of justice, disorderly conduct, or one of several other potential crimes that the officer thinks they can justify by the auditors' insistence that they do not need to identify themselves. One officer, when repeatedly told that he needs to have a crime in order to demand ID, said that the crime was: **Failing to ID yourself.**

These audits are all videoed and put on social media, which can not only be embarrassing for local law enforcement, but in addition, many police officers have cost their communities a substantial amount of money because they did not know the protections guaranteed by the Constitution. They were not familiar with rights afforded the public by the First and Fourth Amendments and proceeded with illegal detentions and arrests.

Because auditors have been illegally detained, arrested, assaulted, had camera equipment confiscated, and even been shot for legally recording in public places, many police departments are now training their officers on the proper methods of handling these types of activities by individuals whose intent is to force (or troll) police officers into situations to determine whether that officer is knowledgeable about the Constitutional rights of citizens who are filming in public. A recent document from the International Association of Chiefs of Police was sent to its members reminding them that "the use of a recording device alone is not grounds for arrest, unless other laws are violated."

Police Reform: Moving From Slogans to Solutions

A recent audit, which occurred in the state of Delaware, highlights the purposeful provocation of law enforcement and how prone to escalation these audits are. The auditor is filming a building (Merck) from a public area, which concerns the building's occupants, and police are called. It bears repeating that court rulings have made the law very clear as it pertains to filming — **individuals are allowed to film anything they can see from a public area.**

Part of the dialog between police and the "First Amendment auditor" is shown below. A link to the entire exchange is included at the end of the transcript of the conversation.

Police: Do you mind if I ask what you're filming for?

Auditor: I am doing a little news story — I'm a journalist.

Police: Do you work for any specific company?

Auditor: I'm just independent.

Police: Do you have any ID on you or anything?

Auditor: No — no I don't.

Police: Well, what's your first and last name?

Auditor: I'm not going to ID — I'm just out here filming.

Police: You're not in any trouble.

Auditor: Yes, I know —that's why I am not going to ID.

Police: You don't have to be in any trouble for me to ID you.

Auditor: That's not what title 11 - 1902 in Delaware says — you have to have some sort of crime that you suspect I committed or am committing. That just blocks the whole getting my ID from me — sorry bud.

Police: Are you from around here?

Auditor: Are you detaining me?

Police: Technically you are not free to go.

Auditor: So you **ARE** detaining me. The law says I can video from public property.

Police: I'm not disputing that — I am allowed to verify who you are to make sure you don't have any warrant or anything like that — okay?

Auditor: Nah —- I'm not going to do that. If we need to escalate — you might want to get a supervisor out here.

Police: Is there any reason you don't want to identify yourself? We are allowed to ID you.

The supervisor arrives and says we need your ID. The supervisor, who clearly also does not know the law, then states that it is time for us to "educate you." The **auditor** then recites the relevant code to the officers about the need to have some sort of crime that you suspect he committed, is committing, or is going to commit.

Auditor: I have no obligation to identify myself — you are escalating this. I do this all over Delaware.

The police officers continue to say they are allowed to identify who he is. They mention that they were called out there for a legitimate reason and therefore they are allowed to demand identification. *(This, of course, is not correct and is somewhat surprising that both experienced officers either did not know the law or chose to ignore it.)*

The auditor then asked the two officers: What if a guy was riding a bike and someone calls and says the rider looks suspicious — are you allowed to demand ID? Both police officers answer that yes they are. *(Again, these are both experienced police officers and they appear to have no idea what the Constitutional constraints on their powers are.)*

The auditor asked for their names and badge numbers and the officers kept implying that they have the right to ID anyone they want if they "got a call."

Auditor: Why are we still here? I don't want to talk to you anymore — I broke no laws.

The officers, to their credit, finally realize that they are dealing with an individual who probably knows the law. It is pretty clear that they were dying to know what the law really is and were somewhat intimidated by the auditor's knowledge. They soon back down. Before they leave though, they insist they did not demand his ID, which is clearly untrue. Their demands were repeated over and over again on the video recording of the interaction.

The link to the entire interaction with the auditor and police officers is here: https://www.youtube.com/watch?v=itLSvnrcHfE

What the Constitutional rights auditors are doing is very similar to how pairs auditing is currently being used to "test" landlords, employers, and lending organizations to see if there is racial inequality in housing, employment, and lending. After reviewing hundreds of "audits" that have been posted to social media, my opinion of these individuals, who have taken it upon themselves to test law enforcement, has changed dramatically. My initial reaction was one of exasperation and sympathy for the police officers who were pulled unaware into the trap that was set. I quickly developed a respect and admiration for those auditors who were calm and professional. Law enforcement may be loathe to admit it, but many of these auditors, at great personal risk, are teaching both police departments and citizens across the country a very valuable lesson about rights that are guaranteed by the Constitution. It bears repeating that the auditors who are being productive, such as the one in the case study mentioned above, are to be admired. There are others, unfortunately, who are an embarrassment to the "auditor movement," are counterproductive, and are dangerous to themselves and police officers who engage them. Having said that, there are also some police officers who immediately go to DEFCON 5 when their demand for identification is politely refused. These individuals should not be involved in law enforcement.

(DEFCON 5 is actually the lowest state of alert and DEFCON 1 is the correct term for highest alert. To be accurate, I should have referred to officers going to DEFCON 1, but because movies repeatedly make the mistake of calling a high state of alert DEFCON 5, I was afraid the reader would misinterpret my point.)

Watch this short clip from social media as an officer responds to a polite refusal from a female auditor to his illegal demand for identification. (She is filming from a public area.) I have never seen a police officer jump to this level of anger so quickly for such a trivial reason. He is clearly unstable, has severe anger issues, and is drunk on his own power. Part of the dialog between the police officer and the female "First Amendment auditor" is shown below. A link to the entire exchange is included at the end of the partial transcript of the conversation.

Officer Lacy: DO YOU HAVE PERMISSION TO BE ON THIS PROPERTY???

Auditor: How are you doing today? Can I get your name and badge number?

Officer Lacy: NO YOU CAN'T!!!
Officer Lacy: I NEED YOUR ID …….PLEASE!!

Auditor: Did I commit a crime?

Officer Lacy: DO YOU HAVE YOUR ID? I NEED TO SEE YOUR ID —- ARE YOU REFUSING TO ID YOURSELF?

Auditor: Did I commit a crime?

Officer Lacy: YOU'RE FAILING TO ID YOURSELF!!

Auditor: Did I commit a crime?

Officer Lacy: YOU ARE FAILING TO ID YOURSELF!

Auditor: Did I commit a crime?

The young woman is then put in handcuffs and detained. The crime? Failing to ID herself. When she tells Officer Lacy that he "needs to have a crime that I'm committing to demand my ID," he replies, "I do — failing to ID yourself." Officer Lacy's logic is impeccable: The crime that allows me to demand your identification is the failure to provide identification. ???????? The young woman auditor was charged with several crimes — unresolved at the time of the publication of this book. This was a clear and dangerous abuse of power and it is quite evident from the video that Mr. Lacy does not have the knowledge, temperament or maturity to be a police officer.

You can watch the interaction here:
https://www.youtube.com/watch?v=Uf_-hoKntL8

Police officers must have mandatory training as to how the Constitution applies when law enforcement interacts with the public. A surprising number of police officers do not know or understand the laws that determine when citizens are required to present identification and when they are not required to identify themselves.

Chapter 6

In order to prevent the violation of the rights of citizens guaranteed by the United States Constitution, police officers must have significantly better training to ensure that they understand the differences and legal limitations they are subject to when taking part in the three types of encounters they have with the public.

The first type of encounter is referred to as a *consensual encounter.*

A consensual encounter **does not require a crime or even the suspicion of a crime** in order for it to take place. In this type of encounter, the officer initiates the conversation and does not use commands, intimidation, force, or threats. The individual who is approached by the police officer may be asked questions that the individual has the right to refuse to answer.

The hallmark of a consensual encounter is that the individual engaged by the police officer:

- Must feel free to leave
- Is not required to identify him or herself either verbally or with a driver's license
- Can stop the conversation at any time

If an officer restrains an individual's freedom of movement in such a way that a reasonable person would feel they must comply, the consensual encounter has turned into the second type of encounter, which is called an *investigatory stop.* **(It is also known as a** *Terry stop.***)**

In an investigatory stop or *Terry stop*, the Supreme Court has ruled that police may briefly detain an individual who they reasonably suspect is involved in criminal activity. In this type of stop, there must be **reasonable suspicion** that the person has committed, is committing, or is about to commit a crime. This type of stop is very different from a consensual stop because in an investigatory stop, the individual:

- Is not free to leave
- Is required to identify him or herself either verbally or with a driver's license

Because citizens of the United States have a Constitutionally guaranteed Fifth Amendment right to remain silent, a police officer cannot compel an individual to engage in a conversation or answer questions. The key aspect that allows law enforcement to move from a consensual encounter to an investigatory stop is the requirement that there is a well-founded, articulable suspicion of criminal activity. An officer's hunch or suspicion that an individual has committed, is committing, or is about to commit a crime is not sufficient to escalate a stop to the investigatory level.

Because it is not lawful for police officers to conduct an investigatory stop without reasonable suspicion of criminal activity, it is absolutely essential that police training not only make it very clear to police officers what the differences are between a consensual encounter and an investigatory stop, but also to enlighten officers about the consequences to their careers if they detain individuals without:

a well-founded, articulable suspicion of criminal activity

The third type of police encounter involves an arrest.

In order to make an encounter move to the level of an arrest, a police officer must have probable cause that an individual committed a crime. An officer makes an arrest by physically restraining a person or by using their authority in order to show that the individual is not free to leave. The key term here is **probable cause**. Probable cause is the legal standard that a police officer must have in order to make an arrest, conduct a personal or property search, or obtain a warrant for an arrest. Probable cause is a stronger standard than reasonable suspicion and because of that it requires facts or evidence that would lead a reasonable person to believe that a suspect has committed a crime.

Case Study

August 24, 2019   Aurora, Colorado

Twenty-three-year-old Elijah McClain was in the process of walking home from a convenience store when three police officers from the Aurora Police Department approached him (Officer Nathan Woodyard, Officer Jason Rosenblatt and Officer Randy Roedema). They had received a 911 call about a "suspicious person" who was wearing a ski mask and waving his arms around. Mr. McClain, who was listening to music when the first officer arrived, was told to stop walking. Mr. McClain reluctantly stopped, but informed the officers that he had a right to continue walking toward his home. At this point the consensual encounter, which does not require a crime or even the suspicion of a crime in order to take place, has legally ended. In order for the police officers to legally escalate the consensual encounter with Elijah McClain into an investigatory stop or Terry stop — which would allow them to briefly detain him — they must reasonably suspect that Mr. McClain is involved or was involved in criminal activity. Because the law requires substantially more suspicion to move beyond the initial consensual encounter, the Aurora police officers needed to have a clear and precise answer for Mr. McClain if he were to have asked them, "Do you have an articulable reasonable suspicion that I have committed a crime, am committing a crime, or am about to commit a crime? If so, what crime do you suspect me of having committed or am about to commit?" In spite of the fact that Mr. McClain had not committed a crime, and in fact was not in any way suspected of anything more than "being suspicious," officers immediately illegally restrained him.

Mr. McClain, after asserting his right to continue walking, was physically confronted and grabbed by one officer who stated that he had the right to stop him because he looked suspicious. As the other two officers approached, Mr. McClain became very distraught and cried out: "I am an introvert, please respect the boundaries that I am speaking. Leave me alone."

As the three officers became more aggressive in their restraint of Mr. McClain, he begged the officers to release him and tried to get out of their grip. He was eventually taken to the ground and warned that they would release a dog on him if he didn't calm down. When additional officers arrived, Mr. McClain was eventually restrained by the use of choke holds. During the struggle, Mr. McClain stated several times that he could not breath. He told them his name. He told them he had an ID and was not armed. He told the officers that his house was "right there." He sobbed, he vomited and then apologized: "I wasn't trying to do that, I just can't breathe correctly."

After Mr. McClain was subdued, Aurora first responders were called, and even though he was listless and clearly incapacitated, paramedics injected Mr. McClain with a high dose of a powerful sedative called ketamine. Shortly after the injection, Mr. McClain went into cardiac arrest and died after spending several days on life support.

It is very clear that these police officers lacked the legal grounds to stop McClain and to forcefully detain him. While the initial consensual encounter might have been justified, the immediate escalation into an unlawful and unprofessional investigatory stop and arrest that led to an innocent man's violent death shows the dangerous consequences of inferior police training. The officers in this situation failed miserably in their understanding and implementation of the differences and legal limitations that they are subject to when they have encounters with individuals. Mr. McClain's rights that the officers violated are clearly defined rights that have been enshrined and guaranteed in the United States Constitution and reinforced by years of case law.

After the tragic death of Elijah McClain that was caused by an appalling misuse of authority, an inexcusable ignorance of the law, and a total and unconscionable lack of common sense, let's take a more personal look at the young man who died at the hands of these police officers. Was he possibly a gang member walking home? Was he in and out of jail for years? Was he a violent individual whom the police were forced to deal with in a violent manner? Let's look closely at the consequences of improper and abusive policing in the death of Elijah McClain by taking a peak into Mr. McClain's life and reviewing what friends thought of this young man who died at the age of 23:

- McClain worked as a massage therapist.

- He taught himself to play both the guitar and the violin.

- McClain believed that music would help soothe the anxiety of cats and dogs so he often spent lunch breaks at local animal shelters, putting on concerts for the animals.

- Friends knew him as gentle: "I don't even think he would set a mouse trap if there was a rodent problem," one friend was quoted as saying.

- Another friend: "He had a child-like spirit … He lived in his own little world. He was never into, like, fitting in. He just was who he was."

- Another friend explained that the mask that drew the attention of the police was something that helped him manage his social anxiety. "He would hide behind that mask. It was protection for him, too. It made him more comfortable being in the outside world."

- Another quote from a friend: "He was the sweetest, purest person I have ever met."

- "He was definitely a light in a whole lot of darkness."

After hearing about the kind of person Mr. McCain was and how many hearts he touched in his short life, let's take a peek into the culture of at least part of the Aurora Police Department. The consequences that the officers faced after Mr. McClain's death are easily researched and will not be addressed here except for the case of Jason Rosenblatt. Mr. Rosenblatt was fired, not because of his involvement in Mr. McClain's death, but because of an incident that happened at a memorial for Elijah McClain in October of 2019. A police officer at the memorial posed for a photograph with his arm wrapped around another officer's neck. This was clearly an imitation of the choke hold used during the submission of Elijah McClain that likely contributed to his death. Not only were both officers smiling, but a third officer (female) could be seen standing behind them smiling. Jason Rosenblatt was not in the photograph, but after the photograph was texted to him, his reply was "haha." The police chief stated that the reason Rosenblatt was fired was because of "his utter inability to do the right thing here."

This is a video that shows some of the police interactions that led to the death of Elijah McClain:

https://www.youtube.com/watch?v=s78szANlt-c

Case Study

September 22, 2019   Loveland, Colorado

Preston Sowl, a disabled 60-year-old man and his wife were leaving a local bar when they saw a trapped man lying under a motorcycle that had crashed. Because the damaged motorcycle was blocking the parking lot exit and because the rider was clearly injured, Sowl and a few other bystanders lifted the bike off the man.

Shortly after the motorcycle was moved, Loveland Police Officer Paul Ashe arrived on the scene and started questioning Mr. Sowl about the crash. Mr. Sowl told the officer:

"I don't know what happened, I'm not talking to nobody."

Officer Ashe immediately escalated the encounter by threatening to arrest Mr. Sowl for obstruction if he would not talk to him — even though it was clearly within Mr. Sowl's constitutional rights to refuse the officer's demands to answer his questions. (A citizen cannot be charged with obstruction — or any crime — for refusing to answer questions from police.)

Remember that Officer Ashe was called to the scene because of an injury accident and the injured motorcyclist was lying on the ground. Officer Ashe's entire focus immediately pivoted to the good samaritan "with an attitude."

Officer Ashe and other officers soon arrested Mr. Sowl. His arms were twisted forcefully behind his back due to his failure to submit to an arrest. He was eventually thrown to the pavement and his hands were cuffed behind his back. Mr. Sowl ended up being badly injured in the takedown. He dislocated his shoulder, suffered bruises to his head, knees, legs, arms, wrist, and reinjured a torn rotator cuff that had been recently repaired. Because of the serious damage to his shoulder, Mr. Sowl was eventually forced to undergo a complete shoulder replacement.

Officer Ashe cited Sowl for obstruction of a peace officer and resisting arrest, but the charges were dismissed. Mr. Sowl recently settled with the Loveland Police Department for approximately $300,000. None of the officers involved in the incident were disciplined.

The fact that Officer Paul Ashe so aggressively violated the fundamental guarantees of the First, Fourth, and Fifth Amendments and his willingness to escalate the original consensual encounter with

Mr. Sowl into a physical confrontation where Mr. Sowl's shoulder needed reconstructive surgery, is a testament to his immaturity, unprofessionalism and lack of training. Officer Ashe clearly does not have the temperament, competence, character, or ethics to remain in law enforcement.

Officer Paul Ashe's body camera footage of Preston Sowl's illegal detainment and arrest:
https://www.youtube.com/watch?v=cv_oTM80PIA

When body camera footage and other recordings of police interactions with individuals are studied, it is very clear that many police officers have an insufficient understanding of the differences and legal limitations police are subject to when they take part in consensual encounters, investigatory stops (Terry stops), and arrests. Police officers across the country are constantly confusing what type of stop they are engaged in and many times they are caught on film taking part in a consensual encounter, but are treating it as an investigatory stop. Extensive training needs to reinforce the fact that: An officer may briefly detain an individual only when they reasonably suspect they are involved in criminal activity.

Important note: Looking suspicious is NOT a crime! If you are ever asked for your ID because you "look suspicious," simply ask the officer: Is being suspicious a misdemeanor or a felony?

In order to prevent the violation of the rights of citizens guaranteed by the United States Constitution, police officers must have significantly better training to ensure that they understand the differences and legal limitations they are subject to when they take part in the three types of encounters police officers have with the public. They must ask themselves: Is there a reasonable suspicion that the person has committed, is committing, or is about to commit a crime? In addition, the officer must be able to articulate what that crime is.

Chapter 7

No-knock or "knock and wait" warrants should NOT be used for drug seizures. Their use should be limited to instances that involve imminent danger.

Because no-knock or "knock and wait" warrants conflict with the right to self-defense and the castle doctrine, both of which permit the use of firearms against perceived intruders, these types of forced entries to private property can lead to the use of deadly force by police and private citizens who believe their home is being broken into. Injuries and deaths of innocent people — including police officers — have happened and will continue to happen if significant policy changes are not made.

Case Study

March 13, 2020   Louisville, Kentucky

Breonna Taylor, a 26-year-old emergency room technician at a local hospital, was shot to death by plainclothes officers who broke down her door while serving a no-knock warrant at one in the morning. Taylor's boyfriend, Kenneth Walker, who said he heard pounding at the door and thought an intruder was breaking in, grabbed his legally owned handgun. Walker and Breonna Taylor then walked cautiously toward the front door. As they approached, the door was violently broken down and, fearing for his life, Mr. Walker fired one shot. In response to the single shot, three of the seven officers who were part of the warrant team fired a total of 32 rounds throughout the apartment. Breonna Taylor was hit by six bullets and died in the hallway of her apartment.

The raid on Breonna Taylor's apartment, which was part of a narcotics investigation, was not only compromised by poor planning and poor execution, but it was clearly a raid that never should have happened. The warrant was based almost exclusively on the dubious theory that Breonna's apartment was possibly storing narcotics shipped by an old boyfriend to her apartment. A Louisville postal inspector said that he had been asked earlier to investigate whether Ms. Taylor's home had been receiving suspicious mail. After an investigation by the postal service, no evidence of wrongdoing was found, yet a no-knock violent raid still occurred, which led to the death of the 26-year-old woman. A subsequent search of Taylor's apartment found no drugs.

Mr. Walker was subsequently arrested and charged with assault and attempted murder for the shot that wounded Louisville Metro Police Sergeant Jonathan Mattingly. (Charges were eventually dismissed later in the year.) Many activists believe that it is very likely that if Breonna Taylor's death had occurred as recently as several years ago, Mr. Walker would have spent decades in jail.

Case Study

July 31, 1997   Brooklyn, New York

The New York City Police Department received a tip from a man who shared an apartment with two Palestinian men. He told police that the men had an explosive device and were going to bomb the New York subway system. Based on that information, police officers conducted an early morning raid at the Brooklyn apartment. As police broke through the door, one of the men reached for an explosive device and both men were shot. During a search of the apartment, police recovered a bombing device that was constructed of four pipes. Each pipe was loaded with black powder, was operational and only lacked a timer. The ready-to-detonate bomb that was intended to bomb a crowded Brooklyn subway could have easily killed hundreds of New York subway riders if police hadn't taken quick and decisive action.

In the Breonna Taylor case, where officers conducted a home invasion to "search for drugs," the warrant was obtained based on a convoluted story of Breonna's apartment possibly storing narcotics that would eventually be sold at a different location. Even if it was important to "apprehend" Breonna, the officers knew, or should have known, that Breonna left her apartment each morning at 7:00 to travel to her place of employment. She could have easily been served the warrant at that time as opposed to breaking her door down in the middle of the night. It is difficult to come away from this tragic story without getting the impression that the way this interdiction was planned and executed was very likely much more about an adrenaline thrill for the involved officers, instead of safe effective policing.

The number of no-knock warrants granted by courts has grown from approximately 1500 in 1980 to an annual number that is now approaching 100,000. It is very difficult to continue to justify the use of these types of warrants in light of the tragic death of Breonna Taylor, and therefore, all jurisdictions should immediately limit the use of no-knock warrants or knock and wait warrants to "imminent danger" cases such as the one used properly in the 1997 raid in Brooklyn, New York, where police officers prevented **imminent deadly criminal activity.**

Chapter 8

The use of K-9 units should be dramatically scaled back.

The sensitivity of a drug dog's nose has never really been questioned — they have a phenomenal ability to detect scents. The major concern with drug dogs is their reliability, because in addition to an ability to detect scents, they also have an exceptionally strong tendency to respond to subtle cues by their handlers. A study by researchers at UC Davis confirmed that the performance of drug dogs is affected by these subtle cues — either intentional or unintentional. The study suggested that when the handler believed that there were drugs present, the dogs "alerted" at a significantly higher rate than when handlers did not believe drugs were present.

The researchers at UC Davis who conducted this experiment recruited 18 handler-detection dog teams from several law enforcement agencies. The dogs involved in the study had anywhere from 2 to 7 years of experience, and their handlers had up to 14 years of experience working with drug dogs. The study, which took place in a church, involved the dogs being taken to several locations and given the opportunity to "alert" or "not alert" to drugs. The dogs ended up alerting over 200 times.

How accurate were the drug dogs — the same type of dog that has given police probable cause to search tens of thousands of vehicles each year? Well, they were not very accurate. In fact the results were very disturbing and hinted at a very unpleasant fact: The constitutional rights of tens of thousands of individuals may have been violated because of inaccurate drug dog "alerts." As mentioned earlier, drugs were detected over 200 times by the K-9 units, but no drugs were in the church at all! **The dogs "hit" incorrectly over 200 times.** This study showed in a dramatic way that a handler's expectations can significantly impact a drug dog's performance. Some studies have even found that dogs are more likely to have false alerts when the vehicle being "sniffed" belongs to a Black or a Hispanic person. In these cases, it is probable that the dog is picking up unconscious cues (and racial bias) from the handler.

When you couple the fact that a drug dog "alert" gives police probable cause to search a vehicle without an owner's permission, with the knowledge that many studies have shown that drug dogs have error rates of approximately 50 percent, you are setting up routine, egregious violations of Fourth Amendment rights. It is the duty of law enforcement to balance the prevention of criminal activity with the right to freedom from unreasonable searches afforded citizens by the Constitution, but when the probability of a drug dog's alert being accurate is similar to a coin toss, it becomes very clear that the pendulum has swung too far and the rights of citizens are being seriously threatened.

Drug dogs are currently being used in a way where police departments around the country are motivated to use a dog that "hits" and not a dog that is accurate. You might ask what consequence is there for law enforcement when one of the most cherished rights in this country — *The right of the people to be secure in their persons, houses, papers, and effects, against unreasonable searches and seizures* — is violated by an inaccurate "alert" from a K-9 unit? I'll save you hours of research — **NONE!** There are no consequences whatsoever for a police officer or department when a drug dog has an inaccurate alert and an individual's car or truck has its contents thoroughly searched. Because there are no repercussions when inaccurate K-9 hits give police probable cause to subject tens of thousands of Americans to invasive and clearly unconstitutional searches each year, police departments must have an incentive to make only legitimate searches or a substantial disincentive to search the cars of innocent Americans.

The courts and the citizens of our country put so much value on the Fourth Amendment that we have been willing to release known murderers from prison because the evidence used to convict them had been seized illegally. The invasive and unconstitutional searches that we are currently allowing to happen because of the misuse of drug-sniffing dogs is not consistent with the value we place on being "secure in our persons, houses, papers, and effects, against unreasonable searches and seizures."

With this reality in mind, the easiest and most effective way to make sure police departments have an incentive to make only legitimate searches, is to mandate a painful disincentive:

Each search where probable cause was established by the use of a drug dog, where no drugs were found, shall lead to the payment of $10,000 to the individual whose Fourth Amendment rights were violated.

This policy change would almost certainly limit searches to valid probable cause situations and restore the Fourth Amendment protections so many people have lost over the past several years. The following stories encapsulate several areas of public concern with law enforcement that involve: Fourth Amendment protections, K-9 units manufacturing probable cause, improper use of force, racial profiling, and community alienation.

Case Study

August 9, 2018   Louisville, Kentucky

Eighteen-year-old Tae-Ahn Lea, who is Black and lives in Louisville's West End, had just graduated from Central High School with several college scholarships. He was Homecoming King and had a job selling new cars at a major dealership. Mr. Lea had never been arrested or been in trouble before.

Tae-Ahn Lea borrowed his mother's car to go out for a slushie on August 9, 2018. On the way home, he was pulled over by Louisville Police Officer Kevin Crawford for making "a wide turn." Lea followed orders and even asked for permission before he reached into his pocket to get his license. The officer then grabbed him by both wrists and pulled him from the car. Crawford asked Lea several times if he had any drugs or weapons. Lea repeatedly told him no. Crawford then illegally frisked him, even though there was nothing to indicate that Lea was "armed and presently dangerous." Finding nothing on Lea, police asked permission to search his car. After Lea declined, he was handcuffed and a drug-sniffing dog was brought to the scene. After circling the car, the K-9 "alerted" to contraband inside Lea's mother's car. Because the dog "indicated drugs," police had probable cause to search the car. The police officers, in addition to searching the car, also went through Lea's wallet.

Tae-Ahn Lea was released 30 minutes later, but not before the police officer asked him questions such as:

- *"If you don't mind me asking, why do you have like this negative view toward police?"*

- *"What's the deal? Whatever happened in your life...can you give me a good explanation?"*

After the teen explained that he is an honor student, has a scholarship to college and has a good job, the police officer, without having a clue as to the irony of his question, followed up with:

"So what's the problem? Why are we in this situation?"

The police, who had clearly racially profiled Mr. Lea, kept the young man in handcuffs on the side of the road for almost 30 minutes and then had the temerity to ask, "Why do you have a negative view of the police?" This traffic stop was clearly an egregious misuse of police authority, not only because of its obvious violation of Mr. Lea's Fourth Amendment rights, but also because of how disproportionate the escalation of the law enforcement interaction was when juxtaposed with the alleged offense of "taking a wide turn." This kind of bad policing is not only morally wrong, but it undermines law enforcement's effectiveness and also leads to generations of community distrust. If Mr. Lea didn't have a negative view of the police before this traffic stop, Officer Crawford sure provided a reason for the young man and his family to have one now!

Tae-Ahn Lea's 30 minute interaction with police is here. The title of the video is: *Police handcuff Black teen for a wide turn and then tell him to "quit with the attitude."*

https://www.youtube.com/watch?v=LtQG0JlCORI

Case Study

August 20, 2020   Russellville, Arkansas

Arkansas State Police Trooper Steven Payton stopped Marion Humphrey Jr., a 32-year-old Black third-year law student, on Interstate 40 near Russellville, Arkansas. Trooper Payton pulled over Humphrey because "he changed lanes too quickly." Mr. Humphrey, the son of a retired judge, was moving from Fayetteville to Little Rock in a rented U-Haul truck and, because he couldn't get the driver's window down on the unfamiliar vehicle, was asked to exit the truck. Then, without any apparent reason except for the possible fact that Mr. Humphrey was Black, Trooper Payton quickly and dramatically escalated the traffic stop by calling for backup and a drug-sniffing dog.

The officer asked the student about when and where he rented the vehicle and interrogated him about when and where he planned to return it. When Mr. Humphrey inquired as to why he was being questioned so aggressively, Trooper Payton responded:

"Yea, because you're super nervous. I'm trying to figure out why you're so nervous." Keeping all aspects of this traffic stop in mind, it should be clear that Mr. Humphrey might have been nervous for several obvious reasons that seemed to escape Trooper Payton.

Note to an oblivious Trooper Payton: **This traffic stop was conducted three months after police killed George Floyd!**

After the dog arrived, Mr. Humphrey was handcuffed and placed in the back of a patrol car. The dog was then walked around the perimeter of the truck and unsurprisingly "alerted" to drugs. While Mr. Humphrey sat handcuffed in the patrol car, Payton and three other officers thoroughly searched the U-Haul truck for over an hour and found nothing. Two hours after the traffic stop was initiated, Mr. Humphrey was given a warning for careless driving and was allowed to leave.

Fortunately, the dashcam video from Payton's patrol car captured the entire two-hour traffic stop and clearly showed that there was no valid legal basis to escalate the encounter with Mr. Humphrey beyond a simple traffic infraction. Using the video record of his detainment, Marion Humphrey went on to file a lawsuit against Trooper Payton for the actions he took on behalf of the Arkansas State Police.

"Through this lawsuit, I seek to stand up for my constitutional right to be free from police targeting because of the color of my skin. I seek not only justice for myself, but also, by taking this stand and challenging the traumatizing conduct of the Arkansas State Police and Trooper Payton, I hope to show others that we will not stand by and tolerate racist police practices in our home state of Arkansas."

Humphrey's attorney, Connor Eldridge, went on to say: "I am proud to represent my friend Marion Humphrey Jr. in standing up for his constitutional and basic human rights to be free from racist and illegal treatment due to the color of his skin. It is inexcusable that the Arkansas State Police and Trooper Payton conducted themselves in this manner, stopping Marion because of his race and arresting him, leaving him handcuffed in the back of a police car for over an hour, while they tossed around his possessions, finding nothing."

Marion Humphrey's traffic stop is worth studying because it contains several levels of police misconduct: Racial profiling, inappropriate K-9 searches, Fourth and Fourteenth amendment violations, and illegal detainment. Trooper Payton has repeatedly justified violating Mr. Humphrey's rights because "he appeared nervous." It bears mentioning again that the night Mr. Humphrey was pulled over on a dark Arkansas interstate by an armed white state trooper, who was soon joined by three other armed troopers and a K-9 unit, was less than:

Three months after police killed George Floyd.

The courts will eventually decide whether Marion Humphrey's traffic stop and illegal search involved racial profiling. An important point to keep in mind is that this stop was egregious on many levels — only one of which was racial profiling. If it is found that there is **not** a racial disparity when Arkansas State Police Troopers stop and search motorists (which is highly unlikely), this would not in any way exonerate Trooper Payton and the other officers. The actions they took that night were appalling and the Constitutional rights that were violated were grievous, even if racial profiling was not a factor in their actions.

Marion Humphrey Jr. and his traffic stop and illegal search:

https://www.youtube.com/watch?v=7C9xh96xams

Fourth Amendment to the United States Constitution

The right of the people to be secure in their persons, houses, papers, and effects, against unreasonable searches and seizures, shall not be violated, and no Warrants shall issue, but upon probable cause, supported by Oath or affirmation, and particularly describing the place to be searched, and the persons or things to be seized.

Chapter 9

Law Enforcement in the United States needs more training and better training.

In 1977, shortly after the death of my father, I drove with four of my siblings across the Midwest on our way to Canada for a wilderness canoe trip. It would be an opportunity to bond and grieve for our father who died of cancer at a fairly young age and we were looking forward to a relaxing vacation to try to relieve the stress of the previous year. As we drove on Route 80 across Iowa, we were in the right lane following a large motorcycle at a speed of about 70 mph. A car passed us on our left at a moderate speed and as the driver pulled back into the right lane, she did not notice the motorcycle and drove directly into it.

The motorcyclist, who was not wearing a helmet, was sent flying by the impact and hit the roadway on his left side with his head clearly making direct contact with the pavement. I immediately stopped and pulled off onto the grass next to the roadway, asked my younger siblings to stay in the car, and exited my vehicle to see if I could help.

As I approached the scene, it was clear that the motorcyclist was severely injured. His leg was almost certainly broken near the hip and he also had suffered significant head trauma — he not only had a very disturbing wound, but was also experiencing serious cognitive impairment. He tried to talk, but could only grunt out sounds and gibberish. He was also attempting to stand up and walk. The only medical training I possessed at that time was unfortunately limited to basic first aid that I had learned as part of a summer job as a wilderness canoe guide. It was very clear that the man had brain damage and the only help I could render was to try and hold him down until medical help arrived in order to keep him from further damaging his broken leg.

The man was very strong and it took all my energy to keep him from moving as he struggled to stand up, so I was very relieved to see a police cruiser pull up and an officer step out. I was more than eager to pass this situation off to someone who knew what they were doing, so I asked him to please help me hold the man down until an ambulance arrived. The police officer's next two sentences have stayed with me for the past 44 years and have even influenced the way I currently look at law enforcement:

Police officer: *"Maybe we should let him get up and run it off."*

In response to the man's grunts and gibberish, the officer turned to the crowd of people who had stopped to see if they could help and said:

Police officer: *"He's a deaf-mute, does anyone know sign language?"*

The lack of training that the police officer had in basic first aid was startling. I knew next to nothing about treating serious injuries, but I at least knew:

- You don't move a severely injured person until help arrives.

- If part of a person's skull is caved in and he cannot form words, you are almost certainly dealing with brain damage, not someone who is hearing impaired.

It is of course unfair and unreasonable to let this one incident color my view of law enforcement, and I know that intellectually, but imagine the 18-year-old Black high school student who was pulled over for "making a wide turn" and ended up handcuffed for half an hour while several armed police officers searched his car? What about the young man who was pulled over for a seatbelt violation and had a gun pointed at his head? Will they ever view law enforcement as legitimate and fair? Will their friends? Will their family? This tendency to hold onto "negative impressions" makes each new incident of police abuse much more serious than the initial outrage due to the fact that each new episode undermines a community's longterm faith and trust in law enforcement.

One of the reasons I share this story is that it draws attention to the lasting impact of a negative interaction with a police officer. Another reason is that my experience with this particular police officer highlights the consequences of a deficiency in law enforcement training in one specific area — first aid. We ask police officers to deal with so many different areas which include, but are certainly not limited to:

- Violence

- De-escalation

- Mental health issues

- First aid

- Domestic issues

- Apprehending criminals

- Investigating crimes

- Self-defense

- Firearms training

- Understanding laws and how they apply to individuals that police engage

- Operating police vehicles

It is just not acceptable to think that we can properly train our law enforcement personnel in 21 weeks, which is currently the case — especially when other countries, without the gun and violence issues that are present in the United States, feel that their officers need close to 200 weeks of training before they are prepared to face the challenges and responsibilities of upholding the law.

As mentioned earlier, it is not right to take an anecdote from one experience with one officer, and from it make sweeping generalizations and assessments about law enforcement. That is not my intent. The point is to show the real world consequences of inadequate training in one specific part of law enforcement — rendering first aid. There are of course countless examples of competence and training issues across all occupations and professions and in the interest of fairness, I will share a story where my trust in the medical establishment was also somewhat damaged. This experience led me to a place where I do not have full trust in what I am told by doctors without following up with my own research.

When I was a college student, a friend and I went camping and both had ticks imbedded in our legs. When we returned to college, my friend became deathly ill and was hospitalized with Rocky Mountain spotted fever. Shortly thereafter, I also became very ill and told my doctor about the ticks and about my friend who was currently hospitalized with Rocky Mountain spotted fever. I then asked if I could be tested for it. His response was, "Who is the doctor here?" and refused to order a test. (Maybe some ego control training would have helped.)

To make a long story short, I remained very sick and decided to go to another doctor. This doctor readily agreed that it would be smart to test for Rocky Mountain spotted fever. The results: **Positive for Rocky Mountain spotted fever**

I found out later that untreated Rocky Mountain spotted fever has a mortality rate of 30%. The lack of ego control training by my original doctor was certainly dangerous and could easily have led to my death!

America trains its police officers, as mentioned earlier, for an average of 21 weeks, while several European countries train officers for 200 weeks, require a three-year degree, and are very selective as to who they accept for their program. In Norway for example, only 15% of the people who apply for their police school are accepted.

Due to these stringent requirements and the extraordinary amount of training, Norwegian police officers are for the most part viewed as elite. Because they are taught that the most effective way to gain legitimacy and authority is not by instilling fear in the population, one of their major goals is to maintain the respect and approval of the public. In addition to the extensive training of their police officers, Norway also extensively uses medical experts and psychiatric specialists to assist police officers when they are dealing with individuals who are suspected of suffering from mental illness. The United States, by comparison, often treats people with mental health issues and drug addiction as criminals and does not realize that some law enforcement interactions require a healthcare response instead of a criminal response.

There will be three areas of training that will be discussed in this chapter. Case studies will be used to highlight specific areas of need that cry out for additional training:

1) Common sense and de-escalation training
2) Racial profiling and racial bias training
3) What we can learn from successful police forces in other countries

Common Sense and De-escalation Training

Case Study

August 2, 2020   Aurora, Colorado

Brittney Gilliam, a young Black woman, drove to a nail salon with her 17-year-old sister. Also in the car with them were Gilliam's 6-year-old daughter and two of Gilliam's nieces, ages 12 and 14. When the group realized the salon was closed, they sat in their parked car looking on Gilliam's phone for another salon that might be open. Suddenly, one of Gilliam's nieces spotted police approaching their car with their guns drawn and she screamed. Seconds later, and at gunpoint, police officers ordered the adults and children to exit the car and lie down on the ground.

Video of the incident shows three of the four children face-down on hot pavement, handcuffed, and screaming in fear. One officer attempted to handcuff the 6-year-old girl but the handcuffs were too big for her small wrists. She was wearing a pink crown and crying for her mother. The 12-year-old pleaded with the officers to be allowed to hug her sister, who was lying next to her.

Gilliam was also handcuffed and put into a police car and told by Aurora police officers that the reason her family was being detained was that they were in a stolen vehicle. Gilliam knew that the car was not a stolen vehicle and repeatedly asked the officers to check her license and registration — they declined her request.

The family was held for about two hours until a sergeant arrived. It turns out that Brittney Gilliam was in fact correct when she forcefully told officers that her car was not stolen. The five terrified occupants of the car were approached with guns drawn, removed from their car, handcuffed, and forced to lie on hot asphalt, all because police officers did not follow procedures.

The incident began when Gilliam drove through an intersection that was equipped with a license-plate reader that scans the plates of passing vehicles and compares each plate with a database of stolen or wanted vehicles. If a stolen or wanted vehicle matches the scanned plate, the machine takes a picture of the passing car and automatically sends it to the local police department. Gilliam's license plate number matched that of a stolen motorcycle with Montana plates, but Gilliam was driving an SUV with Colorado plates.

The Aurora police officers, who violently accosted Gilliam's family, failed to look up the plate number in the National Crime Information Center. If they had, as policy required them to do, they would have realized Gilliam's SUV was not the stolen motorcycle.

There are two very clear and disturbing conclusions that any dispassionate viewer can take from analyzing this incident:

1) The Aurora Police Department inadequately trains its officers.

2) The police officers involved in this stop were operating at such a remarkably high level of incompetence and so lacking in even a modicum of common sense that they should be immediately fired and held legally accountable for their actions.

Even though the officers made a glaring error when they failed to double check the "stolen vehicle" plate number with the National Crime Information Center, they quickly compounded their mistake as they approached the vehicle they thought was stolen. It should have been immediately clear that Ms. Gilliam and the 6, 12, 14, and 17-year-old girls in the SUV posed no danger to anyone. The officers ended up dehumanizing and traumatizing helpless children and the adult with them, who was heartbroken that she was put in a position where she could not protect the children with her.

What might be the most disturbing aspect to this entire episode is the fact that five police officers could stand by for this length of time and watch screaming, crying children lying on hot pavement and not initiate any kind of modification to their tactics. It is clear that Aurora police officers have been trained to draw their weapons when they approach a stolen vehicle, which is not an unreasonable policy, but when a different scenario presented itself, the police officers should have been able to react and change their actions. That did not happen here, either because of racial bias, incompetence, or a combination of both.

Two videos that show Brittney Gilliam's experience with the Aurora police officers:

https://www.youtube.com/watch?v=MZeaTN50W2k

https://www.youtube.com/watch?v=nXSWb7oKBpo

Racial Profiling and Racial Bias Training

There must be significant and innovative training by law enforcement departments to address and mitigate the amount of, and the effects of racial profiling and implicit racial bias in policing. I will not be addressing the type of training needed for two reasons:

- I am a 68-year-old white man from Iowa.

- I am not qualified to comment on, and therefore I do not wish to comment on, changes that are needed that might lead to an end to endemic and structural racism in American society.

What I do offer in this publication is a compilation of areas where law enforcement needs policy changes and significant improvements to the training their officers receive. Several of the case studies that have been presented so far, show poor policing that is almost certainly due to racial profiling and bias. In this chapter, I will point out several additional examples that underscore the need for training and education. Again, I will not address the **type** of training needed for the reasons given above. All policing changes advocated in this book should decrease the amount of racial profiling and racial bias in minority communities as a byproduct of those improvements.

Case Study

Nov. 17, 2018   Cincinnati, Ohio

Jerry Isham, an African-American realtor with 32 years experience, was showing Anthony Edwards a house in a Cincinnati neighborhood. The two men entered the residence using the lock box on the door that Isham had access to while Mr. Isham's 9-year-old son waited in the realtor's car. Meanwhile, a retired Cincinnati police officer who was visiting nearby, called 911 to report that "Two black males forced the front door (of the home) open."

Shortly after the 911 call, nine police officers appeared outside the house and demanded the men step outside with their hands up. One female officer had her gun drawn and yelled, "Hands up!.......Tell your friend to come out too, hands up."

Anthony Edwards (client): *We have an appointment to view the home.*

Male police officer: *People saw you were forcing your way in. That's why we're here.*

Anthony Edwards (client): *No, no, no look, they just white people calling the goddamn police doing this bullshit right now. Man, I ain't even going to buy this house.*

Female police officer: *How did you's get in?*

Anthony Edwards (pointing at the realtor): *He's a realtor!*

Female police officer: *Turn around. Until we can confirm, turn around.*

Without so much as asking for identification, the female police officer handcuffs the realtor, Mr. Isham, and reaches into one of his pockets and finds business cards showing that he is indeed a realtor. Unbelievably, she then continues searching Mr. Isham and finds a driver's license and a realtor ID card. **Even after finding a driver's license and a realtor ID card,** another officer continues escalating the humiliation and pats down Mr. Isham's body, including his crotch. They continue the interrogation:

Female police officer: *Who did you arrange this with? Where's the key?*

While Mr. Isham is being questioned, Anthony Edwards is also handcuffed and spends the time he is detained arguing with the other officers about being racially profiled and is understandably very angry. The female police officer, even after seeing that Mr. Isham is clearly a realtor — **as he said he was from the very beginning** — continues to leave him in handcuffs and continues questioning him about a key.

Female police officer: *Do you have the key to the lock box or is it in there? Which pocket is it?*

Mr. Isham: *I don't know. (Clearly angry, disgusted and humiliated)*

The female officer continues illegally searching a handcuffed Mr. Isham — unzipping pockets and reaching into pockets. She finally takes the handcuffs off.

Female police officer: *Sorry about that sir. We can only go by what is reported to us.*

The City of Cincinnati eventually apologized and settled with the realtor and his client and agreed to pay the men $151,000. In a statement, Cincinnati City Manager Patrick Duhaney said, "The city regrets this extremely unfortunate and unnecessary situation. Mr. Isham and Mr. Edwards did nothing wrong."

Video of Mr. Isham and Mr. Edward's interaction with Cincinnati police officers:

https://www.youtube.com/watch?v=Ny2MSKeV_xg

Case Study

Marlin Texas Police Department

In this case study, James Jones is detained in his own yard for "looking suspicious" while two police officers threaten to arrest him for not providing identification. The video begins with Jones and his fiancée asking why the two officers think they look suspicious for simply walking out of their house. The two officers huddle to discuss the situation as Mr. Jones pulls out his camera to narrate.

Mr. Jones: He just came into my yard, violating my rights, trespassing. It's total harassment right here, guys. See, I'm beginning to feel afraid for my life now. Do you have a search warrant to be on my property?

Police officer: I do not, but listen to me — if you can just provide this information for me — your IDs — if you live here

Mr. Jones: I'm not providing you nothing — as a matter of fact, get off my property if you don't have a search warrant — I'm asking you nice.

Police officer: And I was asking you nice as well.

Police Reform: Moving From Slogans to Solutions

Mr. Jones: All I'm saying is that if you don't have a search warrant — the paperwork — to be on my property ….. What crime do you suspect me of committing?

Police officer: The only crime I have right now is the failure to identify.

Mr. Jones: Okay, Okay………..38.02 failure to identify…….one must already be under arrest for a crime that he has committed…… what crime have I committed?

Police officer: Failure to identify

Mr. Jones: Oh, that's not a crime — it only becomes a crime when …..once one has already been lawfully …..(He then quiets down his fiancée.) Be quiet, be quiet………Let me educate this one………Let me educate him. 38.02…….failure to identify only become a crime when one has already been lawfully arrested for a crime……..let me give you an example sir…… since I don't already know who you is.

Police officer: What about detained?

Mr. Jones: Huh…….what am I being detained for?

Police officer: You are being detained because of your suspicious activity.

Mr. Jones: No…..No……. What penal code? — You have to name a penal code that I have committed that is the crime…name a crime I have committed …..you hear me? Name a crime that I have committed other than being Black and walking down this driveway.

Police officer: You were detained for suspicious behavior.

Mr. Jones: If you don't know your job, do not…………..you're dealing with the wrong one, that's why you guys are mad at me…..cause you

106

won't be handling me like you handle the other ones…..cause I'm on top of my game…..I know you see the gold teeth and the tattoos and you think you are dealing with another plain regular Black guy….no player…..wrong one….let me educate you guys today …

Mr. Jones then says he will Google the statute (38.02) and he then reads it to the officers:

(a) A person commits an offense if he intentionally refuses to give his name, residence address, or date of birth to a peace officer who has lawfully arrested the person and requested the information. (b) A person commits an offense if he intentionally gives a false or fictitious name, residence address, or date of birth to a peace officer who has: (1) lawfully arrested the person; (2) lawfully detained the person; or (3) requested the information from a person that the peace officer has good cause to believe is a witness to a criminal offense.

Jones then goes on to explain that if he had stolen something, they may have articulable and reasonable suspicion to detain him, but that standing in his yard was not a reason for a "lawful detainment." The two officers again ask Mr. Jones to give them his name and date of birth. He refuses to back down and continues to exercise his right to be free from unreasonable searches in his own yard. A short time later, the two officers have a quick discussion and decide they have had enough and leave without acquiring an identification from Mr. Jones.

The clear racial profiling that occurred here is very disturbing, but the lack of training and understanding of basic laws that must be followed during an encounter with an individual is appalling. The one positive aspect to this incident is that the officers, for the most part, kept their egos in check. They did not escalate the interaction into violence and knew when they were outclassed.

Mr. Jone's video of his encounter with the two police officers:

https://www.youtube.com/watch?v=LRBxW3PJw5k

Dealing with mental health issues in the United States and what we can learn from successful police forces in other countries

The first two case studies that will be presented in this section address how unprepared and untrained some police departments are to deal with situations that concern children and mental illness. The final case study is presented to give an example of a United State's police officer in a very liberal city whose training is clearly deficient. This officer was involved in possible racial profiling, the use of excessive force, a failure to de-escalate a situation, and an inability to learn from her mistakes. She forcefully arrested an elderly veteran who was walking in downtown Seattle using a golf club as a cane — as he had done for years. It turns out that he was not mentally ill, but the officer had no way of knowing that at the time she confronted the man and arrested him. If he had happened to have mental health issues, the confrontation may have ended up far worse than it did. The Seattle Police Chief fired the officer saying, "She violated department policies regarding bias, discretion, and de-escalating confrontations."

The chapter will end with some areas of law enforcement in other countries which can serve as instructive examples for America.

Case Study: Police interactions with children

November 24, 2018   Albion, Michigan

Da'veon Cieslack, a teenager with cerebral palsy and mental health issues, disobeyed his grandmother and went outside after sunset. Mr. Cieslack's grandmother, who had been taking care of him since he was three years old, was finding it increasingly more challenging to manage her grandson's outbursts and other mental health issues as he grew up. She relied on the police to get Da'veon to cooperate and they were typically very patient and gentle with him.

That night, the young man was near his grandmother's garage when Officer Tyler Collins decided to handcuff him and put him in the back of his police car. When Mr. Cieslack continued to resist cooperating, Officer Collins threatened to put him in a juvenile detention facility, then punched him several times, and pepper sprayed him — all while the young man was handcuffed.

*Officer Collins and the Albion Police Department were very aware of Mr. Cieslack's mental health issues because they had been out on calls involving the young man **38 times** over the past four years. Eusebio Solis, who is the Calhoun County prosecutor's chief assistant said, "They had been to his home numerous times. They were familiar with him. But more importantly, they were familiar with his mental condition. He should not have been treated as a criminal. He should have been treated as a patient."*

Officer Collins was fired. Da'veon Cieslack's grandmother has filed a lawsuit against the Albion Police Department for 10 million dollars.

Police training programs nationwide typically spend, on average, 168 hours teaching officers about the use of force, weapons, and defensive tactics. Mental illness and how to deal with related issues — 10 hours.

Case Study: Police interactions with children

January 19, 2021   Rochester, New York

Elba Pope, the mother of a nine-year-old girl, called police during an argument with her spouse when her young daughter became "unmanageable." When her fourth-grade daughter continued to get out of control, she asked police officers to call mental health services. Body camera footage show officers restraining and admonishing the girl as she repeatedly cried and called for her father. As the officers struggled in the snow to put the young girl in the back of a police cruiser, they told her they were losing patience. They eventually were able to handcuff the nine-year-old girl, and when she failed to follow commands to place her feet inside the police car, they pepper-sprayed her directly in the face.

During her 16-minute wait in the car, the young child cried out repeatedly that she wanted her dad and said that her eyes were burning. Handcuffed in the back of the patrol car, she called out:, "Please don't do this to me — it burns!" One officer responded, "You did it to yourself, hon."

The girl then cried out in pain, "It's burning too bad!" to which an officer replied, "It's supposed to burn. It's called pepper spray." The girl begged the officers to remove the handcuffs because the liquid was running into her mouth and repeatedly asked when the ambulance would arrive to clean the pepper spray out of her eyes.

The lack of training, judgement, and common sense that was on display here is absolutely stunning. To actually believe that it is appropriate and/or helpful to pepper-spray a small child who is not compliant is abhorrent and should be cause for immediate termination. The officers involved were suspended pending the completion of an investigation. The family announced that they plan to sue the City of Rochester.

Case Study

July 9, 2014   Seattle, Washington

William Wingate, a 69-year-old African-American veteran, usually takes a 10-mile walk around Seattle each day with a golf club that he uses as a cane. As Mr. Wingate waited patiently for a light to turn at a crosswalk on Capitol Hill, Officer Cynthia Whitlatch of the Seattle Police Department pulled up in her cruiser and detained Mr. Wingate claiming that he, "swung the club in a threatening manner, striking a stop sign, while she was driving past in her patrol car."

The two engaged in a heated verbal exchange with Officer Whitlatch yelling and repeatedly demanding that Wingate "put down the club." Wingate continued to refuse to drop his golf club and forcefully denied that he swung the club while Officer Whitlatch vehemently claimed that he swung the golf club at her and declared that her "dashcam video will prove it." Mr. Wingate was eventually arrested with the assistance of Officers Christopher Coles and Ben Archer and booked into jail for investigation of unlawful use of a weapon and obstructing a police officer. He spent the night in jail and called it the "most miserable night" in his life.

During her altercation with Mr. Wingate, Officer Whitlatch declared that her dashcam video would prove that Mr. Wingate "swung the club in a threatening manner, striking a stop sign, while she was driving past in her patrol car." The dashcam showed no such thing. The officer's dashcam video was definitive: Mr. Wingate never acted in an "aggressive or threatening manner." City prosecutors dropped the obstruction charge and agreed that the misdemeanor weapon's charge would be dropped in two years if Wingate met conditions set by the court. Prosecutors later moved to dismiss the entire case and the city ultimately apologized to Mr. Wingate for his unlawful arrest and six months later they returned his golf club.

Whitlatch's actions led to a strong condemnation from the community and also led to a February march of protesters who carried golf clubs as canes. Seattle Police Officer Cynthia Whitlatch was eventually fired by Police Chief Kathleen O'Toole, who labeled the officer's actions as biased and overly aggressive policing. Officer Whitlatch's "biased and overly aggressive policing" also cost Seattle's taxpayers over 1.3 million dollars to settle a lawsuit Mr. Wingate brought against the city.

In an ironic twist, it came out later that two months after Whitlatch's arrest of Mr. Wingate, she posted a controversial comment on her Facebook page in response to the riots that occurred after the police killing of Michael Brown in Ferguson, Missouri. In the post she criticized "black people's paranoia for assuming whites are out to get them."

Officer Whitlatch's illegal arrest of a 69-year-old veteran:

https://www.youtube.com/watch?v=I4huLib-c8c

What can we learn from other countries?

What police training practices and political policies are Nordic countries and other European countries utilizing that might serve as instructive examples for America? Let's first look at the number of murders that result in an arrest in Nordic countries and compare it to the United States:

Iceland: 100 percent
Finland, 99 percent
Norway: 97 percent
Sweden: 83 percent
United States: 62 percent

The arrest rate for murders, which is sometimes offered as a testament to excellent policing in Nordic countries, is not a completely fair way to judge police effectiveness because after all, Iceland averages fewer than one murder per year! Nordic success at solving crimes, though, does appear to play a major part in their low crime rate. They focus on catching offenders and, because virtually all serious crime is in fact punished, criminals know that there will be consequences for their actions. Research is also very clear about the need for consequences for those who break the law: **criminal impunity drives crime.**

The fact that serious crime is almost always punished is not the only reason that Nordic countries experience a relatively low level of criminal activity. Other reasons include excellent police training and the fact that Nordic countries provide material security to almost everyone in society — diminishing the impact of inequality, which research has consistently shown is connected to violent crime.

Nordic prisons are also very different from American prisons. Nordic prisons have an emphasis on education, worker training, and entertainment instead of punishment — although punishment certainly is an element of their prisons. One reason Nordic countries seek to provide more opportunities for inmates is to try and ensure that convicts are not turned into hardened criminals in prison. They appear to be succeeding because recidivism rates in Nordic countries are approximately half of what they are in the United States.

Let's move on to the education police receive in many European countries and compare and contrast that training to what is received in the United States. When it is examined closely, the contrast in the different approaches to law enforcement training between the two areas of the globe is astonishing. Mississippi's newly hired police officers get approximately two months of training while six months is typical for basic law enforcement education in several large cities in the United States. Compare that to Germany where police recruits are required to spend two and a half to four years in basic training to become an officer.

The short training requirements of American police departments make it extremely unlikely that anything more than the basic fundamentals of police work will be taught. Many critical and complex areas of law enforcement, such as dealing with mentally challenged individuals, substance abuse, de-escalation training, and Constitutional law are usually not adequately taught in the overwhelming majority of American police academies because of the fact that there is just not enough time.

The second significant difference between European and American police departments is both the philosophy that is instilled during training and the philosophy new police officers are expected to follow in their law enforcement work after they complete their training. In the

United States, the majority of police departments and police academies stress a "take charge and dominate the situation" attitude, while the European focus is usually on de-escalation and striving for legitimacy through community support.

When you look at police training in Europe and then scrutinize areas where law enforcement is deficient in the United States, it is evident that one solution is significantly longer and more rigorous officer education that would allow police who leave our academies to be better able to deal with and be much more knowledgeable concerning:

- Mentally challenged individuals
- People suffering from substance abuse
- De-escalation training
- Ego containment
- Constitutional law

Law enforcement personnel must have increased and more effective training to address three major areas where many police officers across the country have exhibited clear and compelling deficiencies: racial profiling, alternatives to use of force, and de-escalation tactics. When becoming a hairdresser in the United States requires 2000 hours of training and the mandatory training for police officers is approximately 750 hours, something is seriously wrong.

Chapter 10

The body camera or dashcam recording of every interaction officers have with the public must be routinely audited, not only to monitor the demeanor and professionalism of officers, but also to ensure that officers' actions are consistent with what they write up in their incident reports.

Case Study

May 27, 2019 Phoenix, Arizona

A car containing two adults and two small children had just parked at an apartment complex in Phoenix, Arizona. An officer approached the car with his gun drawn. Inside the car were an adult male, a pregnant female, and two children (ages four and one). The police officer pointed his gun at them and yelled out, "I'm going to put a cap in your fucking head!" As other police officers approached the car, a very pregnant Iesha Harper told them that she had a child on her lap and could not put her hands up. After she told an officer that the door was broken and would not open, his response was:

"You're going to fucking get shot!"

After Iesha Harper exited the car, a bystander's video showed an officer trying to grab the one-year-old child from Harper's arms, slightly injuring the child. She refused to release her child to the officer or place him on the hot pavement as ordered, but eventually she handed both children to bystanders. She then was handcuffed and placed in a police car.

Two witnesses filming this interaction were undoubtedly wondering what had prompted these police officers to draw guns on a man and a young mother with small children. Did they rob a bank? Were they being arrested for murder? Maybe they were drug dealers or could they possibly have kidnapped the small children and the police were involved in a heroic rescue? In actuality, the police were responding to a call from the local Dollar Store who informed the police that:

The four-year-old girl "might" have taken a Barbie Doll knockoff without paying for it.

Both adults sat handcuffed in the back of police cars for close to 30 minutes before a lieutenant came and defused the situation. No charges were filed, but after worldwide outrage, one of the officers was eventually fired and the City of Phoenix settled a lawsuit with the family for close to $500,000.

This story highlights the need for constant monitoring of body and dashcam footage of police interactions with the public. It is highly unlikely that the officer who thought the appropriate response to a call about a possible shoplifted Barbie Doll knockoff was to approach a car containing two small children, draw his gun, and yell, "I'm going to put a cap in your fucking head!" was just having a bad day. There is an extremely high probability that if a supervisor studied dashcam or body camera footage of previous interactions this officer had with the public, he/she would find a history of overreactions, escalations, and poor police work.

Bystander video of the incident:
https://www.youtube.com/watch?v=VWAybDJS7ng

Case Study

September 2019   La Paz County, Arizona

*P*hillip Colbert, a 22-year-old Black man, was traveling from Lake Havasu to Parker to meet his father for lunch. He soon noticed a police officer following him and was very careful not to commit a traffic infraction. The officer followed Mr. Colbert for such an extended period of time that Colbert started recording with his phone.

Eventually Deputy Eli Max pulled Colbert over. During the encounter, Deputy Max asked Colbert eight times whether he smoked marijuana. Colbert said no each time. The officer then asked Colbert whether he had any cocaine or heroin, tried to get Colbert to consent to a field sobriety test, and then asked permission to search his car.

Mr. Colbert later said that he declined the sobriety tests, and "I denied him checking the car because I felt as soon as he checked the car, he was going to try to put something in there." Colbert was very upset, not only because the encounter took over 35 minutes, but because of the traffic infraction that led to the very stressful and dangerous traffic stop. Deputy Eli Max detained Phillip Colbert because:

he had a pine tree air freshener dangling from his rear-view mirror.

Mr. Colbert ended up filing a complaint about Officer Max's behavior with the La Paz County Sheriff's Office. After the air freshener incident made local news, a young couple told the local news station about a similar incident that happened to them. Officer Max interrogated the couple for over an hour without cause and then brought in a drug dog to search the couple's vehicle. Eli Max was eventually fired. It is unclear whether Officer Max had a functioning body camera during the stop with Mr. Colbert, but it was fortunate he was able to film the encounter and expose the obvious racial profiling and unprofessional policing that took place during the illegal pretextual traffic stop.

Phillip Colbert's interaction with Officer Max:

https://www.youtube.com/watch?v=_NqZnm7wQeg&t=20s

Case Study

September 25, 2017   West Liberty, Iowa

Bryce Yakish was riding his motorcycle near West Liberty, Iowa, when he was pulled over for speeding by Iowa State Patrol Trooper Robert Smith in what appeared to be a routine traffic stop. The officer's dashcam shows Mr. Yakish pull his motorcycle over, calmly dismount, and then remain standing with his hands by his side. For no apparent reason, Trooper Smith immediately escalated the interaction. He exited his patrol car and then ran at Mr. Yakishr with his gun drawn and pointed at Mr. Yakish.

Smith then assaulted the motorcyclist by striking him in the helmet with his hand, which knocked Mr. Yakish and his motorcycle to the ground. The officer then placed his knee on Mr. Yakish's neck and roughly handcuffed him. Yakish was then arrested, charged with eluding law enforcement, and was forced to spend the night in jail. Mr. Yakish, who suffered a neck injury during the assault, lost his license because of the arrest and had his motorcycle impounded.

When a prosecutor viewed the dashcam video of the traffic stop, it became clear that Mr. Yakish stopped immediately after Trooper Smith activated his patrol car's lights and siren. All charges were dropped. After the dashcam video of the assault and inappropriate arrest of Mr. Yakish was released, numerous other allegations of misconduct against Smith were scrutinized.

Mr. Smith left the Iowa State Patrol in 2018 after a 30-year career and was hired as a police officer in the town of Durant, where Smith again was accused of using excessive force. (He has since resigned.)

In 2019, Mr. Yakish filed a lawsuit against the State of Iowa and former Iowa State Patrol Trooper Robert Smith claiming that Smith assaulted and falsely arrested him and then fabricated the eluding law enforcement charge. In April of 2021, the State of Iowa settled the lawsuit and agreed to pay Bryce Yakish approximately $250,000 from state general tax funds (Iowa taxpayers).

If dashcam and body camera video of Iowa State Patrol Trooper Robert Smith had been routinely monitored, he would not have been able to commit as many assaults and deprive so many motorists of their constitutional rights. His assault on Mr. Yakish was horrifying on many levels:

- The assault was unprovoked.

- It was clearly the action of an angry, out of control bully who enjoyed dominating other people.

- Trooper Smith knew the assault was on camera and either didn't care or thought he would get away with it.

- He was not immediately fired.

- He was hired to work as a police officer in another town.

The most disturbing aspect to this assault is the fact that after a prosecutor viewed the dashcam video of the traffic stop and dropped charges against the motorcyclist, *he did not immediately charge Officer Smith with assault.* The dashcam video very clearly shows an assault on a private citizen by a police officer. Officer Smith was allowed to resign and move on to another town and work in law enforcement.

Video of the assault and false arrest of Bryce Yakish:
https://www.youtube.com/watch?v=sXRCtL9HxBA

Routine monitoring of how police officers interact with the public will not only help weed out officers whose personality and demeanor make them unsuitable for law enforcement, but will also help lessen the amount of racial profiling in policing. The feedback and training officers receive from the increase in supervision and monitoring will also reinforce what is taught through implicit bias training.

Chapter 11

Every police officer in this country, from the smallest town to the largest city, must have a functioning body camera. It is often said that body cameras and dash cameras are there to protect police officers and the public. This is only partially true. The main purpose of cameras is to protect, preserve, and record the truth.

Case Study

December 28, 2016   Walnut Ridge, Arkansas

Adam Finley of Smithville, Arkansas, was stopped by Officer Matthew Mercado of the Walnut Ridge Police Department because he was on property that belonged to the Burlington Northern Santa Fe Railway Company and the officer wanted to know why he was there. Finley, who was wearing a BNSF Railway jacket, explained that he worked for the railroad and showed Mercado his railroad identification badge. Mercado, who thought that Finley had an "attitude," quickly escalated the situation by cursing, threatening, and shoving Mr. Finley. Mr. Finley was pushed into his truck door, forcefully handcuffed, and then unlawfully detained. Officer Mercado eventually removed the handcuffs and freed Finley without citing him for any infraction. As Finley was being released, Officer Mercado threatened to shoot him with a taser, "Next time, you will ride the lightning."

The outrageous treatment that Mr. Finley endured, courtesy of Officer Mercado, did not end there. When Finley went to file a complaint at the Walnut Ridge Police Department, it was instantly decided that he deserved several citations for refusal to submit to arrest and obstructing governmental operations. These citations were written by a different Walnut Ridge officer by the name of Matt Cook with the full knowledge and permission of Police Chief Chris Kirksey.

Adam Finley disputed the charges and was eventually tried and acquitted of all charges. He subsequently filed a lawsuit naming as defendants Officer Matt Cook, Police Chief Chris Kirksey, Officer Matthew Mercado, Walnut Ridge Mayor Charles Snapp, and the city of Walnut Ridge. The city eventually reached a settlement with Adam Finley for $57,500.

The importance of body camera footage was evident after Officer Mercado turned in his incident report — a report that even though it was full of lies, was the evidence the prosecution would use in Mr. Finley's trial.

The abuse that Mr. Finley endured was outlined in his written complaint and lawsuit. The accuracy of Finley's memory was evident when Mercado's body camera footage was finally viewed. There was no audio for the first 30 seconds of the video, but even though Mercado said that Finley immediately had an "attitude," Finley's facial expressions did not convey an attitude problem in the short amount of time the audio was off.

When the audio did turn on, Finley's communication was far from aggressive as Mercado's report suggested. Mercado's report stated that, "Before I was able to introduce myself, the driver began asking me 'What the hell did you pull me over for?' " Mercado then claimed that he asked several times for Finley's driver's license and proof of insurance before Finley complied. Mercado further claimed in his report that he noticed "Mr. Finley was doing something with his right hand under the center console of his truck. It was making me quite uncomfortable. At that point, for safety purposes, I asked Finley to step out of the vehicle — he refused. He continued to complain and tell me that this was the 'stupidest shit ever.'"

Because body camera footage was available and told an entirely different story than Officer Mercado's written report, Mr. Finley's trial ended with his acquittal. Because the body camera footage was so damning and Officer Mercado's behavior was indefensible, Walnut Ridge quickly agreed to settle Mr. Finley's lawsuit for $57,500.

Walnut Ridge is fortunate that was all they had to pay. The law enforcement personnel whom Mr. Finley was forced to deal with acted in a way that was not much different than what you might expect from an inner-city gang or a group of mobsters.

Officer Mercado's "style" of policing is one of the main reasons that some communities and individuals view police officers as tyrants. Officer Mercado did nothing egregious when he first initiated his "consensual encounter" with Mr. Finley and asked why he was out by the railroad tracks — having a truck in that area WAS unusual and the reason why it was there did need to be investigated. It bears repeating that Officer Mercado was initiating a consensual encounter and **NOT** engaging Mr. Finley in a Terry stop because there was no traffic infraction and, in addition, the officer could **not** have had reasonable suspicion that Mr. Finley had committed, was committing, or was about to commit a crime. After explaining why he was on railroad property, Mr. Finley willingly produced his license and railroad identification, even though he was not required to by law. The fact that he cooperated beyond what the law required to help alleviate Officer Mercado's suspicions makes the officer's verbal and physical assault on Mr. Finley even more unacceptable.

Adam Finley and Officer Mercado's interaction:

https://www.youtube.com/watch?v=Q5gBZw4Ev-s

Case Study

July 26, 2017   Salt Lake City, Utah

William Gray, a 43-year-old full-time truck driver and a part-time reserve police officer, was severely burned in a July 26 head-on collision between his semi and a pickup truck that was fleeing from the Utah Highway Patrol. Mr. Gray, who was in a comatose state, was transported to the University of Utah Hospital. Shortly after Mr. Gray arrived, several Salt Lake Police Officers, including Detective Jeff Payne, entered the emergency room area and asked for a blood sample from the patient. The on-duty nurse, Alex Wubbels, informed the officers that their request did not meet the hospital's legal requirements — the very same legal requirements to which the Salt Lake Police Department had previously agreed:

Before blood could be drawn, ONE of the following conditions must occur:

- *The patients must be under arrest at the time of the blood draw.*

- *A warrant for a blood draw must have been issued.*

- *The patient consents to the blood draw.*

Because none of the requirements were applicable to Mr. Gray (the patient), the nurse, with support from her administrator, informed the officers that the hospital could not draw a blood sample from Mr. Gray. In video of the encounter with police, Nurse Wubbels can be seen in Detective Jeff Payne's body camera video holding her phone while the detective appears to be talking to an administrator through Ms. Wubbels's phone:

Detective Jeff Payne: *She is the one who has told me no.*

Hospital administrator: *Yeah, sir, but you're making a big mistake. Right now you are making a huge mistake and are threatening a nurse.*

The detective then stops the conversation with the administrator and grabs at the nurse to arrest her. She backs away and screams and the detective forcibly grabs Ms. Wubbels and puts her in handcuffs and takes her out to his police car. After spending 20 minutes in the police car, she is released without being charged.

After an investigation, Detective Payne was fired by the police department and his watch commander was demoted. Alex Wubbels went on to file a lawsuit against Salt Lake City and the University of Utah. In October of 2017, both sides agreed to settle the case for $500,000.

News story of Nurse Wubbels's arrest:

https://www.youtube.com/watch?v=ulARU2uRBoo

Every police officer in this country, from the smallest town to the largest city, must have a functioning body camera. It is often said that body cameras and dash cameras are there to protect police officers and the public. This is only partially true. The main purpose of cameras is to protect, preserve, and record the truth.

Chapter 12

Because court rulings have made it clear that the public is allowed to film the police, police officers must be trained to react to a camera in the same way they would react to a person watching them.

Recording their own interactions with police or the interactions of others with police is not only a citizen's legal right, but because filming preserves the truth, it is also essential to justice.

Hundreds of police officers are continuing to inappropriately confront people who are legally filming, which has led to those officers receiving reprimands, being fired, or sometimes even being charged with criminal acts. Police interference with a citizen's right to film usually starts with a demand to move farther away from the crime scene because "you are interfering with my investigation" even though the filming is taking place well away from where the police are working.

Police officers sometimes then escalate the situation by either asking or demanding to see identification. While it can at times be appropriate to politely ask to see identification, a person legally filming is **NOT** required to identify themselves unless the officer has an articulable reasonable suspicion that the person filming is involved in criminal activity. In other words, there must be reasonable suspicion that the person has committed, is committing, or is about to commit a crime.

Case Study

Spring of 2014   New York, New York

Jason Disisto was standing outside of a Puerto Rican restaurant around one in the morning when he saw Police Officer Jonathan Munoz start talking to a female friend of his. When Officer Munoz started reaching into his friend's pocket, Disisto asked to borrow another friend's phone so he could record the interaction. Before Mr. Disisto could begin recording, Officer Munoz noticed that he was about to be filmed and rushed over to grab Mr. Disisto. As Officer Munoz struggled to rip the phone from Mr. Disisto's hand, two other officers joined in. Disisto was soon placed in handcuffs and placed in the back of a police car. As the three officers drove away, the cell phone Disisto had borrowed was thrown out the window.

Even though Disisto was the one attacked and was never aggressive, Officer Munoz wrote in his arrest report that Disisto had crouched in a fighting position and had lunged at him and thrown a punch. Because of the violence that the officer alleged Disisto had committed, he was charged with obstructing governmental administration, disorderly conduct, and resisting arrest. Officer Munoz was certainly aware that filing a false report was a felony punishable by as many as four years in prison, but it is likely he was confident that his narration of the events that transpired that night would not and could not be realistically challenged — after all, there were other police officers there who would back his story.

What Officer Munoz did not know when he wrote his report, the report that directly led to several serious charges being filed against Mr. Disisto, was that the entire interaction which occurred that night between Mr. Disisto and the police officers was caught on the restaurant's surveillance cameras — from three different angles! Prosecutors quickly dropped the charges against Mr. Disisto and he later sued the city in federal court. The city eventually settled the lawsuit for an undisclosed amount of taxpayer money.

In 2017, following a trial in Manhattan Supreme Court, a jury convicted Officer Jonathan Munoz of four felony counts and three misdemeanors. The jury found that Munoz illegally arrested Mr. Disisto in retaliation for his filming of the officer as he inappropriately and illegally searched a woman in 2014. Munoz then lied in court documents about what transpired during his interaction with Mr. Disisto.

Munoz was convicted of several felonies and lost his career, all because he was unable to "handle" being filmed. Several people witnessed his illegal search of the woman, but it wasn't until someone tried to document his actions with a camera that he exploded. Even though it is very clear that there can be serious consequences for police officers when they obstruct the legal right of individuals to film, police are continuing to unlawfully detain or arrest individuals and illegally confiscate their cell phones:

- In an attempt to cover up police misconduct

- In an attempt to cover up recording possible police misconduct

- Simply because police officers are annoyed that they are being filmed

Police Officer Jonathan Munoz's illegal detainment and arrest of Jason Disisto:

https://www.youtube.com/watch?v=Byv8MjMFvag

Case Study

April 12, 2017   Gwinnett County   Atlanta, Georgia

Gwinnett County Police Officer Michael Bongiovanni pulled over Demetrius Hollins, a Georgia college student, for not having a license plate. (The license plate, although not in its normal spot, was in the rear window.) Demetrius Hollins recognized Officer Bongiovanni from a stop he was involved in during the summer of 2016 and reached for his phone to film the traffic stop. Hollins testified that Officer Bongiovanni started yelling and stated that he wasn't going to get any video of this stop and "You're not going to make any phone calls, nobody is going to know about this." Hollins was then ordered out of his car. A bystander recorded what happened next:

As Mr. Hollins exited his car with his hands up, Bongiovanni struck Hollins in the face with his elbow. The video shows that Mr. Hollins was then tased in his back, causing him to fall to the ground. As he lay on the ground, Officer Bongiovanni again tased Mr. Hollins and proceeded to put him in handcuffs. While he lay facedown and prone on the pavement, with his hands securely shackled behind his back, another officer by the name of Robert McDonald came running up with his gun drawn and pointed it at Hollins's head and proceeded to kick Mr. Hollins in the face. Not surprisingly, Giovanni's police report of the incident did not mention the kick to the face or the unprovoked assault on Mr. Hollins.

Bystanders who had witnessed the event called police and told them Bongiovanni used excessive force and had elbowed Hollins in the face while he clearly had his hands up. The witnesses also said McDonald came up to Hollins with his gun drawn and pointed it at Hollins's head. At least two of the witnesses also took cell phone videos during the incident that reinforced their testimony.

After reviewing witness testimony and the cell phone video of the event, the Gwinnett County Police Department dropped the charges against Mr. Hollins, fired both Giovanni and McDonald, and then released the following statement:

"The revelations uncovered in this entire investigation are shocking. We are fortunate that this second video was found and we were able to move swiftly to terminate a supervisor who lied and stepped outside of his training and state law."

In a subsequent news release, the Gwinnett County Solicitor-General said, "The actions of these officers completely undermine their credibility and they cannot be relied upon as witnesses in any pending prosecution." He then announced that 88 other cases in which Bongiovanni and McDonald were the principal officers would be dismissed.

Two years later, Bongiovanni pled guilty to aggravated assault and battery. He was sentenced to 10 years, with six months to be served in work release and the rest served either through home confinement or probation.

Robert McDonald was eventually charged with aggravated assault, battery and violating his oath of office. Even though the video evidence told a damning story, McDonald attempted to spin his kick into Hollins's face as something more benign than what several video recordings clearly showed was a kick: "I thought he could be trying to roll over, kick, potentially pull something from his waistband like I've seen happen in the past. I was hoping to place my foot on Hollins's shoulder to keep him on the ground, but Hollins moved and my foot ended up on his face."

After several hours of deliberations, the jury returned an unanimous verdict finding Robert McDonald guilty of aggravated assault, battery, and violating his oath of office.

The police in both of the previous case studies were subject to the same biases and prejudices that witnesses are subject to, but with a disturbing twist. They knew exactly what happened during their arrests and, if they chose to, they could have honestly reported the truth. Unfortunately, they were motivated to lie, they were able to lie, and they chose to lie.

It is important to touch on how humans form memories and compare that process with how a camera processes an event. The process that occurs when witnesses form memories of an experience is both fascinating and disturbing. As the activities that are being observed unfold, light enters the eye of the observer through the pupil and then hits the retina, the light-sensitive layer of tissue at the back of the eye. Photoreceptors then turn the light into electrical signals that travel from the retina and then through the optic nerve to the brain. The brain turns the signals into images. These images are then interpreted by that same brain that can be brimming with biases, prejudices, preconceptions, fears, and apprehension. In most cases, witnesses **TRY** to recall the details of an incident as accurately as possible, but because of the inherent biases that everyone holds, getting to the unvarnished truth can sometimes be difficult.

Because of the susceptibility of human memory to errors and omissions, courts usually view the credibility of the testimony that emanates from human witnesses as much less reliable than evidence that is presented by "trained and unbiased" police officers. Currently, with the proliferation of cameras — cameras that take in light and record an image that is not subject to biases, prejudices, preconceptions, fears, and apprehension — courts often have before them an unvarnished, unbiased, truthful representation of a specific period of time — a nice thing to have if people have different memories of an event!

Officer Michael Bongiovanni and Robert McDonald's assault of Demetrius Hollins: https://www.youtube.com/watch?v=Sr9svTjeVl8

Conclusion

Police abuse, racial profiling, and systemic racism are causing deep soul-searching in this country. As more and more people from both sides of the political spectrum question the legitimacy, competence, and fairness of police officers, the stability and cohesiveness of our society has the potential to deteriorate. To function effectively, police must not only have the legal authority that is granted to them by government, but they must also gain legitimacy from the communities they serve — which they acquire when those communities feel that the authority that police project is fair, legal, and appropriate for the situation.

The cumulative cost of delaying needed policy changes and improved training and therefore allowing an unacceptable amount of police misconduct to go unchecked will be a continuing erosion of legitimacy. If we choose to go this route and not seriously address the obvious changes that must be made to law enforcement, this lack of vision and initiative will not only negatively impact social order, but in the process, it might possibly lay the foundation for the incremental stripping of freedoms — all in the name of law and order.

After viewing hundreds of hours of dashcam and body camera footage that document police interactions with the public, it immediately becomes clear that police officers in the field break down into three distinct categories:

- Always professional with an accurate grasp of the law and how to enforce it fairly, ethically, and legally. They are open to suggestions and learn from mistakes.

- Need better training in order to ensure that they understand the differences and legal limitations they are subject to when interacting with the public, but have the personality and professionalism to be able to change.

- Conduct themselves in a manner that escalates situations when their authority is challenged. They either do not understand the legal limits that law enforcement must respect or they choose to ignore those limitations. This type of officer is often thought of as a tyrant by citizens whom they deal with, which breeds distrust and alienation from the community, on whose support law enforcement depends. Personality, insecurity or ego issues make it very unlikely that this type of officer can modify their behavior enough to become an asset to a police force and a community. This type of officer should immediately be removed from situations that require dealing with the public.

As this book went into final edit, important examples of police misconduct and training deficiencies that reinforce how important it is to move quickly on police reform continue to make national news. I will include a couple final cases here with links to each particular story.

Williamson County, Texas

Several residents of an apartment building called 911 about a possible case of domestic violence in an adjoining apartment because they heard loud arguing. When police arrived at the apartment, a young woman came outside and insisted she was fine and did not want to talk to the police because "your police force has a really bad reputation." A short time later, Deputy Lorenzo Hernandez grabbed the young woman, and when she screamed, he threatened to tase her. Hernandez along with two other deputies then took the young woman to the ground and handcuffed her.

A routine law enforcement interaction that was supposed to be about a young woman's welfare, turned into a violent escalation where a possible victim of domestic assault, who was not suspected of committing a crime, was violently thrown to the floor and handcuffed. The lack of common sense, professionalism, and compassion is absolutely stunning. How much training is needed to understand that when you are trying to help a possible domestic assault victim, it is not a good idea to assault her?

https://www.youtube.com/watch?v=hV6rJ4j87uM

2013   San Marcos Texas

After Officer Palermo pulled over a car in a downtown bar parking lot, Alexis Alpha, a 22-year-old Texas State University student, walked between the police cruiser and the car that was stopped. For some inexplicable reason, Officer Palermo took offense at where the young woman had walked and stopped her — even though video of that night showed several other people walking through the exact space between the vehicles. Ms. Alpha insisted she had done nothing wrong and began arguing with Palermo. The officer immediately escalated the interaction by grabbing Ms. Alpha's arm. He then took hold of her shoulders and neck and pushed her into the car. Seconds later he slammed the young woman, who happened to be half his weight, face first into the concrete — breaking several of her teeth.

Alexis Alpha was charged with public intoxication, resisting arrest and also a felony charge of obstruction of justice. All charges against Ms. Alpha were dropped a week later after video of the arrest was viewed. Hays County eventually indicted Officer Palermo on a charge of aggravated assault by a public servant because dashcam video of the incident clearly showed Palermo slamming Ms. Alpha's face into the roadway.

When investigators looked at Officer Palermo's conduct during previous arrests, they discovered a pattern of violent escalations and assaults that they should have caught long before Mr. Palermo had the opportunity to abuse Ms. Alpha and others. During an interview with an investigator, Palermo was filled in on what was discovered about his previous record:

"As we've been going through those cases.... do you know what we have found? You like to file resisting arrest... and you file it really... inordinately more than any other officer in this police department. And we find that a lot of these people get hurt."

The first-degree felony that Officer Palerno was charged with could have led to over a decade in prison, but Palermo was never taken to trial, nor was he sentenced to a day in jail. Officer Palermo's abusive history:

https://www.youtube.com/watch?v=OEiuxcFrTe0

I want to again make it clear that I have a great deal of respect for law enforcement personnel who do their job professionally and honorably and that our country owes a debt of gratitude to these dedicated men and women. We ask our police officers to be willing to put their lives on the line in dangerous situations such as intervening in domestic disturbances, dealing with mental illness, apprehending armed individuals, mass shootings, and many other situations that involve violence.

A professionally run police force is an integral part of a properly functioning society, and our communities would be much more vulnerable to chaos and criminal victimization without police.

Here is a final synopsis of the important changes I feel must be quickly implemented:

- Heavily armed officers with guns, tasers, pepper spray, and body armor should not in any way be involved in enforcing minor motorist infractions that can be dealt with by mailing a citation.

- Heavily armed officers with guns, tasers, pepper spray, and body armor should not in any way be involved in enforcing jaywalking, littering and parking laws.

- *Civil forfeiture should never be used without due process of law and should never provide revenue enhancement for a police force, city or community.*

- *Fines and fees should never be used for revenue enhancement for a city, or community.*

- *There must be significantly more training that deals with the limitations and constraints that the First, Fourth and Fifth Amendments have on police officers when they interact with the public.*

- *Police officers must have significantly better training in order to ensure that they understand the differences and legal limitations they are subject to when they take part in the three types of encounters that police officers have with the public:*

    1) Consensual encounter
    2) Investigatory or Terry stop
    3) An arrest

- *No-knock or "knock and wait" warrants should **NOT** be used for drug seizures and should only be used in imminent danger cases.*

- *The use of K-9 units should be scaled back and not used as probable cause generators. In order to dramatically lower the number of warrantless searches, individuals who have had their Fourth Amendment rights violated by an illegal search prompted by an incorrect "alert" from a drug dog should be generously compensated.*

- *More and better training should be mandatory. The United States trains police officers for 21 weeks while many European countries, with much less violence and crime, train their officers for 200 weeks. Mental health personnel must be utilized when it is clear that an individual is in mental distress.*

- *The body camera or dashcam recordings of every interaction officers have with the public must be routinely audited.*

- *Every police officer in this country, from the smallest town to the largest city, must have a functioning body camera.*

- *Police officers must be trained to react to a camera in the same way they would react to a person watching them.*

Here is a final case study that I find both disturbing and fascinating. I could not find an appropriate chapter for it in the book, but I believe that it is important because it demonstrates how government bodies have the ability to slowly take away rights that are granted to citizens under the Constitution if those government institutions are not held to account. This case study is not about a law enforcement action or agency — it concerns an egregious abuse of government power by Oregon's State Engineering Board.

Case Study

Mats Järlström began his interest in traffic lights when his wife became the unlucky recipient of a red light camera ticket in their hometown of Beaverton, Oregon. After studying the formula for the timing of a yellow light in the three light sequence, Mr. Järlström came to the realization that the formula for determining the length of time the yellow light needs to shine needed to be modified because it didn't take into account the actions of drivers who were turning right.

After Mats Järlström talked to several people about his idea, it became apparent that there was an enormous amount of interest in his thoughts on the subject. A local television station covered his theory, traffic engineers wanted to hear about it, and Mr. Järlström even gave a presentation at the Institute of Transportation Engineers National Conference. After Mr. Järlström gave several presentations on his *theory, something very unexpected and shocking occurred — Oregon's Engineering Board announced that Mr. Järlström was not allowed to talk about traffic lights in public until he obtained a state-issued professional engineer license. The Board then levied a fine of $500. Oregon's Engineering Board proclaimed that a state-issued professional engineer license was required before Mr. Järlström could continue publicly sharing his opinion on the safest and most efficient way to program traffic lights. The Board then made it clear that Mr. Järlström would face thousands of dollars in fines and up to one year in jail if he continued to make speeches and continued with his "unlicensed practice of engineering."*

To add insult to injury, the Board also told Mats that even though he has a degree in electrical engineering and has had decades of engineering experience, he was not allowed to call himself an engineer. After the Institute for Justice agreed to take his case, Mr. Järlström filed suit saying that Oregon's Engineering Board was operating as if the First Amendment did not apply to it.

The U.S. District Court for the District of Oregon decided the case in late December of 2018. The federal court entered a permanent injunction:

Mr. Järlström was allowed to speak freely about his traffic light theories and he was allowed to call himself an "engineer." The court, commenting on the Engineering Board's "history of overzealous enforcement actions," also invalidated Oregon's restriction on the title "engineer."

Institute for Justice attorney Wesley Hottot said of the decision: "In a free society, government agencies do not have the authority to rewrite the dictionary. Oregon cannot declare the word 'engineer' off-limits to the thousands of Oregonians who, like Mats, are engineers." Mr. Järlström's story:

https://www.youtube.com/watch?v=Wi4brP0sXSQ

Police Reform: Moving From Slogans to Solutions

Freedom of speech is a principle that supports the right of an individual or a community to articulate their opinions and ideas without fear of retaliation. It is stunning and frightening that Oregon's Engineering Board thought it was appropriate, legal, and ethical to forbid a citizen from giving his opinion on the flaws inherent in traffic lights.

Made in the USA
Monee, IL
28 April 2026

49136485R00079